FOR THE LOVE
OF PERFECTION

FOR THE LOVE OF PERFECTION:

RICHARD RORTY AND LIBERAL EDUCATION

RENÉ VINCENTE ARCILLA

ROUTLEDGE / NEW YORK LONDON

Published in 1995 by

Routledge
29 West 35th Street
New York, NY 10001

Published in Great Britain by

Routledge
11 New Fetter Lane
London EC4P 4EE

Printed in the United States of America on acid-free paper.

Library of Congress Cataloging-in-Publication Data

Arcilla, René Vincente, 1956–
    For the love of perfection : Richard Rorty and liberal education /
  by René Vincente Arcilla.
      p. cm.
    Includes bibliographical references and index.
    ISBN 0-415-91050-1 (cloth).—ISBN 0-415-91051-X (paper)
    1. Education, Humanistic. 2. Education, Higher—Philosophy.
3. Metaphysics.   I. Title.
LC1011.A63   1994
370.11'2—dc20
                                    94-20981
                                      CIP

British Library Cataloguing-in-Publication Data also available.

To my parents, Teresita and René

TABLE OF CONTENTS

PREFACE

When I began to work on this book, my interest in philosophy of education was responding to two events in contemporary American culture. The first was Richard Rorty's critique of analytical philosophy and of the epistemological tradition from which it stemmed. His work helped me to understand why the concerns which first hooked me on the traditional philosophical literature of my college humanities courses, concerns about how I might become a better and happier person by orienting my conduct to a sense of purpose necessitated by my mortality, seemed so disappointingly irrelevant to the profession of mainstream contemporary philosophy. His argument that the turn away from such concerns has led philosophy into an identity crisis, then, felt like a call to come home. It encouraged me to explore how a stronger sense of vocation might be restored to the discipline if philosophers once again aspired to cultivate paths to a more meaningful life, and how such a quest could claim my life.

The second event which clarified my interest was Allan Bloom's critique of recent developments in liberal education. For liberal education to matter to the youth engaged in it, he argues, it should be helping them to learn from and about their longing for intimacy and purpose; when that education increasingly neglected this desire for self-knowledge, it became a frill to be dispensed with in favor of specialized study. His argument helped me to see that what drew me to philosophy was a longing that could not be contained by the attractions of either a particular subject matter or a set methodology. It encouraged me to explore another way of understanding the vocation of a philosopher: namely, to be a liberal learner and not a specialized researcher or teacher.

Rorty offered me a plausible account of why contemporary philosophy is in an identity or "paradigm" crisis, Bloom one of why a similar crisis is befalling contemporary liberal education. And both suggested that the key to resolving these crises is for these two disciplines to concern themselves together with questions about how their participants might harmonize their conduct with the meaning of their mortality. Thus it occurred to me that one way of reforming these disciplines might be to marry them with respect to this central concern, and to elaborate, accordingly, a new paradigm for a philosophy of liberal education.

Of course many things stand in the way of this union, not the least being aspects of Rorty's and Bloom's critiques which work against the quest for self-knowledge. Even as Rorty attacks positivism, his work seems prone to a positivistic impatience with existential mystery. It often summarily discounts any practical need we may have to cope with the ineliminability of such mystery, thereby reducing the scope of what can count as pragmatist thinking. My concerns must, then, fall outside that scope. As for Bloom, there is his infamous politics. Some of it strikes me as incidental spleen that simply digresses from the argument about liberal education. But there is another part, especially where he flaunts a callousness to problems of social discrimination, which does seem rooted in an educational blindness. I would characterize it as an inability to see even the possibility that the texts and practices of a liberal education may have, in addition to their supposed educational uses, unacknowledged or unconscious political ones. More precisely, when educators use such texts and practices to encourage students to find their ideals, they may be also discouraging them from looking for their ideals in other texts and practices, particularly in those which are rooted in oppressed cultures. Such an education, then, perpetuates the myth that those cultures have little to offer, which of course contributes to the disrespect shown them.

Now the guiding intuition behind this book is that we will be able both to combine the strengths of Rorty's and Bloom's critiques into a philosophy of liberal education, and to separate out those parts of their thinking debilitating to such a philosophy, if we can reconcile one of their most prominent differences: that over the value of metaphysical questioning for philosophy and liberal education. Rorty largely blames the European tradition's interest in metaphysics for the paradigmatic dominance of epistemology in modern philosophy, and calls us to cure ourselves of our weakness for metaphysical questions. Bloom, on the contrary, blames the New World's decline of interest in metaphysics for the incoherence and aimlessness of its contemporary liberal education; he reminds us of our venerable need to take those questions seriously. In order to consolidate and build on the insights of Rorty and Bloom, this conflict has to be resolved. Is metaphysics a valid discipline, and can the questions it raises and responds to help us quest for the meaning of each of our lives?

My book tries to answer this. It argues that Rorty was right to bury metaphysics as a positive science, but wrong to presume that this laid to rest metaphysical questions and their compelling hold on us. Like Bloom, I believe that these questions express a real human need; no thinking can ignore them and still call itself pragmatic. But I suggest that we may avoid metaphysical dogmatism, and the hegemonizing forms of social thought which, as in Bloom's work, often accompany it, by appreciating how the questions lead not to any knowledge but to a communion with the question of perfection, to a kind of "negative metaphysics." I develop this suggestion out of a close reading of Rorty's arguments against epistemological philosophy, and for the learning practice he calls conversational edification.

In my reading, I have chosen not to engage extensively the growing secondary literature on Rorty, and to concentrate instead on building a comprehensive interpretation of his work that responds step by step to a line of questioning specifically concerned about the value of metaphysics for liberal education. I have judged it less useful to review controversies about Rorty's logic, scholarship, and politics that lack that concern, and more useful to explain in some detail how this interpretation might make a difference to how we appreciate and respond to the concern. I leave it to others to implicate the interpretation in those controversies; the interpretation will have served its principal purpose if it succeeds in drawing interest and thought to a new possibility for philosophy and liberal education. Indeed, I am quite aware that those acquainted with Rorty's work may find my yoking of his pragmatist arguments to a discussion of perfectionism to be *prima facie* incongruous. By hopefully overcoming that impression, my interpretation should serve to expand the possible significance of his work in a thought-provoking way.

If my thinking is at all plausible and interesting, then readers may want to know more about where it fits in the history of ideas of liberal education and in contemporary debates about that education. In this respect, I must acknowledge a limitation of my discussion. In response to the question above about the role of metaphysics in liberal education, I have tried to develop some suggestions about the desire, aim, and practice of liberal education in a consistent fashion. More work remains to be done to show how this account is kin to, and bears on, the different ideas of other educational thinkers.

Having completed the book, I see that it starts to raise a set of questions which I am yet far from knowing how to answer. Rorty's history of ideas, which he acknowledges was influenced by Martin Heidegger's, suggests that the birth of metaphysics in Plato's thought may have found its dialectical end in Nietzsche's conception of the will to power. If so, then perhaps another way of describing this history is as the failure—adapting a phrase from Hans Blumenberg—of the first overcoming of sophism, for it is as if Nietzsche's critique of Platonism as unacknowledged will to power represents a repudiation of any real distinction between the intellectual and educational practices of Socrates and Protagoras. Of course the work of the sophists and of Nietzsche would have to be compared in depth in order to substantiate this analogy. Were the analogy to be tenable, however, it would draw fresh attention to Socrates' response to the sophists as a potential locus of union and renewal for philosophy and liberal education. Was Socrates right to criticize certain qualities of the sophists' education, particularly their claims to arm students with rhetorical powers of self-assertion in exchange for a calculable fee? Do these qualities characterize contemporary education? If they do and are indeed dangerous, can we develop anew a nonsophistic, philosophical approach to education, especially one that avoids the now apparent sophism of Plato's metaphysics? And in developing such an approach, would we not find especially useful non-Western traditions of thought, such as Zen, with its stress on nothingness rather than form as a sign of perfection? These and related questions appear to me to be intimated in the book, particularly in the last chapter, but it would take another study formulated in different terms to get such questions properly in focus.

Writing this book has been a labor of thanks for so many lessons in friendship in the course of its composition. The book was largely inspired by my experiences in Harry Harootunian's Friday reading group at the University of Chicago. For six years, our critical and wondering conversation perennially transformed my world, and solidified my educational ideals. I am grateful to all the members of that unforgettable community.

I am also grateful to Richard Rorty, who early in my research responded helpfully to my questions.

Two other conversations helped me try to mean what I say here. Stephen Swords challenged me to believe in what I have lived, and Klaus Amburn to live out what I believe.

Sophie Haroutunian-Gordon was one of my most careful readers and provided warm and wise guidance. Philip W. Jackson has been at my side from start to finish, and has never let my thinking rest. From him I continue to learn why I have to make yet another effort to teach.

Jayne Fargnoli has been a supportive and able editor. Anne Sanow, Ray Walker, and Annie West have also extended to this project their expert assistance.

Earlier versions of two chapters in this book are published elsewhere. Chapter One appeared under the title "Metaphysics in Education after Hutchins and Dewey," in *Teachers College Record* 93, No. 2 (Winter 1991). An earlier version of Chapter Six will appear as "How Can the Misanthrope Learn? Philosophy for Education," in *Philosophy of Education 1994*, published by the Philosophy of Education Society.

I could hardly have made it through the process of writing without the support of many other friends and my family. My parents especially, to whom the book is dedicated, blessed me with a trust that outlasted every trial. Finally, I would like to thank Patricia Dahl, friend of my conscience, for the book I did not write.

1

IS THE DESIRE FOR LIBERAL EDUCATION METAPHYSICAL?

Moral Perfectionism's contribution to thinking about the moral necessity of making oneself intelligible (one's actions, one's sufferings, one's position) is, I think it can be said, its emphasis before all on becoming intelligible to oneself, as if the threat to one's moral coherence comes most insistently from that quarter, from one's sense of obscurity to oneself, as if we are subject to demands we cannot formulate, leaving us unjustified, as if our lives condemn themselves. Perfectionism's emphasis on culture or cultivation is, to my mind, to be understood in connection with this search for intelligibility, or say this search for direction in what seems a scene of moral chaos, the scene of a dark place in which one has lost one's way. Here also is the importance to perfectionism of the friend, the figure, let us say, whose conviction in one's moral intelligibility draws one to discover it, to find words and deeds in which to discover it, in which to enter the conversation of justice. With respect to the issue whether virtue is knowledge, whether virtue can be taught, whether to know the way is to take the way, perfectionism's obsession with education expresses its focus on finding one's way rather than on getting oneself or another to take the way.[1]

Every time I read this passage by the philosopher Stanley Cavell, I am deeply moved by its vision of education as a personal path, opened by a friend, back to the moral path one has lost. When I first encountered them, Cavell's words evoked my best experiences as a student and a teacher, words that I realized I had been waiting for for a long time. In response, I resolved to make more intelligible why I felt that this was so, why I recognized in his idea of "moral perfectionism" the rationale and guide not only, as he mainly takes it, for the reading of Emerson, but also for the conversation that composes, in my experience, a liberal education. Excitedly I shared the passage with friends; one of them, apparently as impressed as I was, remarked that it evoked the need for an education in values. "Of course," he added, "the problem remains: Whose values?"

At the time that seemed obvious enough: what educator has not been given pause by current controversies over the values at stake in "multiculturalism" and in "the canon." But now I wonder whether this interpretation of Cavell's passage—one which reads it as implying that students need to learn somebody's or some culture's values—clarifies the appeal to "morality" only at the cost of obscuring the idea of "perfectionism." If we assume that morality in liberal education is a matter of recognizing and imparting certain values, we risk overlooking the moral education we each receive whenever we respond to perfectionist scruples, whenever we are moved by discontent with our imperfect, hypocritical lives, whenever we love something better. Perhaps the polemical will to assert and defend values should be distinguished from the longing to perfect ourselves; perhaps this distinction will throw into relief what is to be desired in liberal education today.

This book seeks to explore this possibility. It is written to reassure teachers (or as I would call them, scholars) and their (fellow) students that the life of self-examination is worth living. It is also written to provoke philosophers of education to consider transforming themselves from social theorists of educational practice—a self-conception expressed, for example, in John Dewey's famous declaration that "philosophy is the theory of education as a deliberately conducted practice"[2]—into fellow liberal learners, fellow conversationalists engaged in questioning themselves before taking things for granted, in order to receive their being at a loss as a present. Suspending any question of comparative merit, we can at least differentiate the philosopher who examines a general, anonymous practice from one who is personally engaged in making her or his mortal self intelligible. The latter, Socratic philosopher conceives of herself or himself as someone who never stops learning, who pursues that learning in public conversation with others, and who liberally resists social pressure to suppress that learning. Her or his *love* of learning, and appreciation of it as a force of redemption, is prior to any commitment to a critical theory. And the writing of such a philosopher would aspire to be less a theory of liberal education, for example, than a record of part of its author's liberal learning, one which may spur the unspecialized reader to reflect appreciatively on the desire that leads to reading, and to a renewed intimacy with what must be *understood*.

What do I mean by a liberal education? Although nothing less than this whole book can be my answer, the following sentence by the political philosopher Michael Oakeshott elegantly starts to identify some of the distinctive features of this education.

> The invitation of liberal learning . . . [is] the invitation to disentangle oneself, for a time, from the urgencies of the here and now and to listen to the conversation in which human beings forever seek to understand themselves.[3]

This sentence draws attention to five characteristics of liberal education. The first is that liberal education is above all concerned with a kind of learning, not teaching. The second is that liberal learning, in this spirit, occurs in response not to a (teacher's) demand, but to an invitation which one is allowed to accept or reject. It is learning appropriate to the free person. The third is that liberal learning invites us to take a moratorium from the demands of practical life. The fourth is that it also invites us to listen instead to a special conversation. Here I would interject an emending reply to Oakeshott in the form of a question, Why cannot liberal learning invite us not only to listen to the conversation but to join it? And the fifth is that what characterizes this conversation is that in it human beings quest, from generation to generation, for self-understanding. What calls you to join this quest, what makes the invitation so attractive, is the recognition that your sense of yourself leaves something to be desired. But there are also bound to be moments, we are wryly warned, when the conversation itself and the reasons for being in it will become incomprehensible.

Why does this conception of liberal education emphasize the activity of learning rather than teaching? The reason may lie in the example of Socrates, who, according to Plato in the *Apology*, disavowed that he was a teacher.

> I have never set up as any man's teacher, but if anyone, young or old, is eager to hear me conversing and carrying out my private mission, I never grudge him the opportunity; nor do I charge a fee for talking to him, and refuse to talk without one. I am ready to answer questions for rich and poor alike, and I am equally ready if anyone prefers to listen to me and answer my questions. If any given one of these people becomes a good citizen or a bad one, I cannot fairly be held responsible, since I have never promised or imparted any teaching to anybody, and if anyone asserts that he has ever learned or heard from me privately anything which was not open to everyone else, you may be quite sure that he is not telling the truth (33a–b).[4]

In keeping with his famous polemic against the sophists, Socrates remarks here that if anyone learns something in the process of listening or replying to him, they do not do so in the context of some contract to be taught a specific lesson for a specific fee. What they learn—or, as he would say, recollect—is up to them; nobody can assume responsibility for this learning but the learner. Indeed, when he converses with others, he is not assuming the role of teacher, but learning with them as an equal, as someone who is motivated by and who proceeds from a scrupulous acknowledgment of his own ignorance. Socrates suggests, then, that the learning proper to a free person should not be bound by the expectation that it can be bought from a knowing superior. Although our institutions are far from being in a practical position to observe this injunction, we can at least partially admit its truth by shifting the burden of a liberal education to the learner.

This depreciation of the role of the teacher roughly distinguishes liberal education from grammar education on the one hand, and vocational or professional education on the other. (Perhaps I should add that I, at least, do not read these distinctions as implying anything about how these educations should be ranked in importance or prestige.) Oakeshott calls the former "school-education," and characterizes it as follows.

> School-education . . . is learning to speak before one has anything significant to say; and what is taught must have the qualities of being able to be learned without necessarily being understood, and of not being positively hurtful or nonsensical when learned in this way.

> Or, it may be said, what is taught must be capable of being learned without any previous recognition of ignorance: we do not begin to learn the multiplication tables because it suddenly dawns upon us that we do not know the sum of nine 8's, nor the dates of the Kings of England because we know we do not know when Edward I came to the throne: we learn these things at school because we are told to learn them.[5]

It is a teacher, of course, who tells children to learn such things (or a parent sending her or his child to a teacher), and who accordingly takes charge of the learning process. We delegate this responsibility to teachers because we assume that most students at this stage of development are not sufficiently motivated, skilled, or discriminating to learn what they need to know on their own. Even when they do become capable of such independent learning, however, they may continue to learn in a setting that is teacher-dominated. This is the case in what Oakeshott calls "vocational education," which trains us for specialized jobs from gardener to lawyer.

> The design of a "vocational" education is to be concerned with current practice and always with what is believed to be known. . . . The significant principle of specialization in this sort of education derives not only from the fact that most learners are concerned to acquire only one skill, but from its being concerned to impart to the learner what may be called the current achievement of a civilization in respect of a skill or practice needed in the contemporary world. In short, a "vocational" education, while it does not absolutely forbid it . . . makes no provision for teaching people how to be ignorant; knowledge here is never the recognition of something absent.[6]

The content to be learned here consists of know-how or knowledge that will enable you to perform a specific task valued by contemporary society. As the task is more or less already defined, so too is the knowledge needed to do it; whether someone is qualified to call themselves a possessor of this knowledge, then, can be clearly determined. The learning process in vocational education accordingly amounts to a transfer of goods from those who possess them to those who do not; it is a process that the teacher is in a superior position to direct. In neither grammar nor vocational education, then, does the learner accept responsibility for her or his own learning. In liberal education, however, the learner finds a direction for learning in the confession that she or he is ignorant about something of crucial importance.

Who am I? In my case, what does the name "René Vincente Arcilla" mean? I answer to it, I ascribe value, need, action, responsibility, and purpose to it—but I am not sure why. It is the answers to these and related questions that the liberal learner feels intolerably ignorant of, and needs the help of others to find. What motivates your efforts to learn is the desire for self-knowledge. Yet what if the others to whom you turn have no way of directly revealing you to yourself; what if they are equally searching for themselves? If there is any hope for liberal learning in such a situation, then it must lie in the power of the conversation as a whole, beyond the control of any single participant, to disclose truths about ourselves surprising to all interlocutors.

Why should the desire for self-knowledge lead the liberal learner into a conversation that is removed from the urgencies of the day? Could not an engagement with those urgencies bring self-knowledge? Certainly it could—but there is an important reason why it may not. When you realize that you lack self-knowledge, that ignorance is apt to appear less like a *tabula rasa*, as if you had no idea of who you were, than like a perplexity that the various self-conceptions you take for granted do not form a coherent whole. Now you probably received these conceptions from people in your immediate world, and they are likely to be charged with the expectations of these people that you will continue to define yourself accordingly. At the same time, however, continued identification with these conceptions threatens you with incoherence. For you to examine and reform them, then, you need some freedom from the expectations of others that insist on them. You need an opportunity to quest after a more coherent, deeper self-knowledge, without this quest being unduly constrained at the outset by urgent demands that you be such-and-such a person for such-and-such practical purposes. Of course it is neither possible nor desirable to remove all such constraints; most of your neighbors would want you, like Descartes, to adhere to some kind of provisional, sensible moral code during your self-examination.[7] But in order to encourage the liberal learner to explore freely possibilities of self-understanding, liberal educators need to suspend at least some of those constraints for a time.

Proceeding from these characteristics which distinguish liberal learning from other forms of education, and proceeding from how these characteristics echo aspects of Cavell's passage above, I can start to imagine the scene of liberal education as follows. A group of learners, chaired by a particularly experienced learner or scholar, sits in a conversational circle. What draws them together, and what animates their talk, is a longing that cannot be confined to resolving an urgent practical issue of the day. Despite the fact that their longing may have been originally prompted by such an issue, its object soon becomes an understanding of each of themselves that is liberated from constraining misunderstandings they have received, misunderstandings that have led them to realize that they have, to some extent, lost their way in the world, or that the world affords them no way to what they love. Such misunderstandings may include originally unproblematic notions of health, normality, success, prosperity, and so on, notions which they may have picked up in their grammar or vocational educations. Since these learners are so lost, they all need each other to help them rediscover a sense of self-direction which they must nevertheless claim for themselves. Hence they have recourse to conversation, to an exploratory, associative, open-ended, tolerant exchange of intimations free from the demand that it issue in conclusions binding on all. Instead, these intimations foster "conversational relationships of acknowledgment and accommodation."[8] And to lift the conversation above familiar constraints, these learners will conduct it in some measure in the foreign terms of texts that come from a distanced past, a futuristic avant-garde, or a different culture, texts which illuminate their world in a new light.

To be sure, there is much about this imagined scene that needs further clarification, and much that appears, lacking further explanation, of dubious educational worth. Who are these people? Where did they come from? Where is this place of learning? Where do they go when they leave it? What do they do? I shall return to this concern about this learning's social context; first, however, I turn to another set of questions regarding the relation between liberal learning and the desire that invites and motivates it, the desire for self-understanding. What causes this desire, with its sense of having lost one's way? Is it a desire that we really need to satisfy? How is liberal learning supposed to satisfy it?

Cavell links the desire for self-knowledge to another, all-too-familiar desire. In response to a lecture by Allan Bloom, Cavell agreed with Bloom on the importance of certain issues for how we understand university education. One moment of agreement concerns:

> . . . the goal of a democratic university education as keeping open the idea of philosophy as a way of life, call it the life of the mind, a name for which might be Moral Perfectionism (Bloom speaks of the longing for completeness . . . [he sees] in the goal a desire for the world's human possibilities, and [is] aware that the aspiration is always threatening to turn into debased narcissism or foolish imitation). . . .[9]

Cavell connects Moral Perfectionism to a longing or desire which Bloom, in *The Closing of the American Mind*, identifies. Indeed, Bloom's name for Moral Perfectionism, so to speak, is eroticism.

> Eroticism is a discomfort, but one that in itself promises relief and affirms the goodness of things. It is the proof, subjective but incontrovertible, of man's relatedness, imperfect though it may be, to others and to the whole of nature. Wonder, the source of both poetry and philosophy, is its characteristic expression. Eros demands daring from its votaries and provides a good reason for it. This longing for completeness is the longing for education, and the study of it is education.[10]

Normally, we understand eroticism to be synonymous with sexual desire and satisfaction. Why would Bloom want to associate it with the "longing for education," and Cavell with the "idea of philosophy as a way of life?" Why would both suggest that the goal of a democratic liberal education is the "keeping open" of such eroticism? Conversely, how could eroticism serve as the motive to liberal learning?

This idea of eroticism was most famously articulated, of course, in Plato's *Symposium*. In it, Socrates learns from Diotima, his teacher in the art of love, that the longing awakened in him by beautiful bodies is more truly, less self-deceptively, a longing for beautiful, eternal, perfect forms of understanding. His eros, being at bottom his ignorance and poverty of self-understanding, orients him ultimately to ideals that do not exist in the physical world, to metaphysical ideas. To respond to eros satisfactorily, he first needs to admit to himself the pit of his need, his blindness, so as to rouse himself to turn toward the light, the wondrous sight, of these ideas of perfection. By living by them, he will come to understand them, and be reassured that they, and his soul which is akin to them, cannot be reduced to mortal, physical beings. Eros thus amounts to the soul's transcendental predisposition to affirm the goodness of the forms we love, our relation to these forms, and our capacity to understand and cultivate rationally this relation.

Plato's text serves as the classic account of why Bloom would associate eroticism with philosophy, the "love of wisdom," and with an education in perfectionist, metaphysical ideals. (Although Cavell is likely to be sympathetic to elements of this account, his Emersonian attitude would probably lead him to displace the interest in ideals onto tropes and passages to a new, next, better self.)[11] It is a conception of eroticism that radically challenges our contemporary assumptions and obsessions about sexual fulfillment. These assumptions threaten to turn eros, in Cavell's words, into "debased narcissism or foolish imitation." Bloom puts the challenge as follows:

> Socrates' knowledge of ignorance is identical with his perfect knowledge of erotics. . . . [But] the sex lives of our students and their reflection on them disarm such longing and make it incomprehensible to them. Reduction has robbed eros of its divinatory powers. . . . There is almost no remaining link visible to them between what they learn in sex education and Plato's *Symposium*. . . . Are we lovers anymore? This is my way of putting the educational question of our times.[12]

Another way of putting it is, Are we philosophers anymore?

Bloom quickly adds, in his peremptory manner, that "the fact that this perspective is no longer credible is the measure of our crisis."[13] Truly this perspective on eros—not to mention philosophy—is bound to sound to contemporary ears half quaint, half crazy. Before leaping to measure some crisis in this sound, though, I wonder if we cannot get clearer about why this perspective so challenges believability. The main hurdles are (1) the claim that the understanding of metaphysical perfections is something human beings actually desire, and (2) the claim that this putative desire may and should find some satisfaction in education. Unless these claims can be made credible, the attempt to look for the satisfaction of eros beyond sexual activity will appear, as it does to many in our time, perverse, self-deceptive, and unhealthy. And as we shall see, there are good reasons to suspect that these claims are beyond belief.

One way to cast the first claim in a plausible light, as well as to clarify the meaning here of metaphysics, is to consider how we might react if tragedy struck someone we loved. Suppose that while you are out walking with a friend, he is suddenly struck by a car. As help arrives, you keep crying out: "Why did this have to happen?!" No one present would understand you to be asking about the physical causes of this tragedy, as if your question could be answered with an explanation that, because the car weighed a certain amount and was travelling at a certain speed and struck an object of significantly less mass, this event had to happen. Most people would take your question to be an expression of horror and grief. Yet later, if you or another were to take that question seriously as a question, it might be rephrased and elaborated as follows: How can this tragedy be part of an acceptable order of things, an order affirmed by your attachment to that person's goodness? What is its reason for being? Why ought it to have happened?

These are metaphysical questions; the meditation on them, and the attempt to answer them, constitutes metaphysics. They do not ask about how the physical world happens to work; rather, they ask about how things and events in it may evoke, and fit into, an ideal order more perfect than its physical manifestations, one which in some sense relates you to this world and makes it good. One example of such a transcendental, metaphysical order is Plato's aforementioned realm of ideal forms, where the invisible idea of the circle, for instance, enables us to see the perfection that circular objects and pictures evoke without being able completely to express; we know what a perfect circle is, despite the fact that it cannot be drawn. Other examples of metaphysical order include Christianity's realm of God's will, Mahayana Buddhism's realm of nothingness, Romanticism's realm of Nature, and so on. Each of these and others were elaborated by thinkers in response to questions like those above; these visions of order enable us to find in even awful events some link to a sense of perfection, such that we may be reconciled, somewhat, to those events and the despair they cause. They reassure us that for everything there is a reason for its being, one which completes our sense of ourselves by finding us a home in an order of things which was only apparently violated.

Tragedy, then, may provoke in us the same half-formed desire to establish the relatedness, goodness, and rationality of all things that we experience in erotic wonder. The need for the above reassurance, then, is one way that the desire to understand metaphysical perfection may be expressed; insofar as we by nature take seriously metaphysical questions as a way to find such reassurance, we should admit that the latter desire actively exists. It is far from certain, though, that we ought to permit ourselves this kind of reassurance or seek to satisfy this desire, for we may be only kidding ourselves, or sweeping worse problems under the rug. Should we promote metaphysical questioning and speculation in our society? In particular, should we promote it in formal education? Moving to the second of Bloom's claims above, we need to ask ourselves: Is this a desire that we should try to satisfy in education?

Such questions stimulated one of the great educational debates of the 1930s and 1940s: that between Robert M. Hutchins, president of the University of Chicago and a principal advocate of the "Great Books" approach to higher education, and John Dewey, the distinguished pragmatist philosopher.[14] Hutchins argued that education, truly conceived, actually depends on metaphysics, and therefore should respond to and promote metaphysical questioning and speculation. Dewey contended that such a metaphysical education would have authoritarian consequences harmful to our democratic values, and so should be discouraged. A reexamination of this debate should illuminate reasons for and against any project to make metaphysics an object of education, let alone the erotic focus of liberal education.

Why did Hutchins, to start with, think that educators, particularly those involved in higher, liberal education, ought to be interested in metaphysical questions? The answer is that such questions direct us to concern ourselves with what is fundamental to living a purposeful life, and so fundamental to any conception of the aim of education.

> How can we consider man's destiny unless we ask what he is? How can we talk about preparing men for life unless we ask what the end of life may be? At the base of education, as at the base of every human activity, lies metaphysics.[15]

Recall the nature of metaphysical questions: they ask why should something be the way it is, that is: Why should human beings live? What is their reason for living? What is their reason for making music? Metaphysics thus includes the study of the nature and purpose of human life, and of the purposes that each of our activities should attempt to achieve in order to be consistent with the essential nature and purpose of everything. Since education is one such activity having its own particular rationale or purpose, the study of what constitutes the true purpose or aim of education is part of metaphysics. Now, however much we may differ about details, we normally agree that the aim of education, in the broadest sense, is to prepare us for life. The aim of the best education, then, would be to prepare us to achieve the purposes, and central purpose, proper to human life. One crucial way it could do that is to help us acquire reliable knowledge of those purposes. Therefore a central aim of education, according to this conception of metaphysics, is to educate us in metaphysics.

> We see, then, that metaphysics plays a double part in higher education. By way of their metaphysics educators determine what education they shall offer. By way of metaphysics their students must lay the foundations of their moral, intellectual, and spiritual life. By

way of metaphysics I arrive at the conclusion that the aim of education is wisdom and goodness and that studies which do not bring us
closer to this goal have no place in a university. If you have a different
opinion, you must show that you have a better metaphysics.[16]

There is something circular about Hutchins's reasoning here, but
before we dismiss it out of court, we should appreciate both how
modest and how powerful it is. Modest, because it does not rest on
any specific, substantial, metaphysical claims; Hutchins restricts its
main premise merely to the possibility of asking and knowledgeably
answering metaphysical questions. Powerful, because from such a
modest premise he is able to deduce, first, that such an inquiry,
whatever its conclusions, would be essential for determining the
aim of education, and second, that fostering the power to engage
in such inquiry should in fact constitute the central aim of education.
Furthermore, his argument appears to tie us up in its clutches: for
us to dispute with this metaphysical conception of the metaphysical
aim of education, we must have an education in metaphysics—
which is precisely Hutchins's point.

But as I mentioned, the argument suffers from circularity; this
becomes especially evident when we consider how easily it could
be used to claim that other disciplines should play an essential role in
education. Do not questions in art history, economics, astrophysics,
physiology, and so on, also promise to inform us about who we are
and why we are here? Why can we not base the aim of education
on any of these fields of inquiry, and insist that to engage in this
inquiry should be the primary aim of education? Yet if we did, then
to dispute with us, Hutchins would have to grant that an education
in such a field is just as essential as any metaphysical one.

This rejoinder, however, sets us up for Hutchins's stronger argument that metaphysics should have a preeminently prescriptive role
in education, one which allows him to specify further the central
focus of metaphysical inquiry. If several disciplines, proceeding from
their own premises and principles, are each capable of formulating
different views of who we are and why we are here, then how do
we determine which view should serve as the basis for our education?
We evidently need to identify those premises and principles which

are general to all disciplines, and to use those to formulate a view of ourselves that unites all other specialized, partial views, insofar as those views may be derived from it. We need, therefore, to inquire into what our disciplines and their views are grounded on. Yet the need for such inquiry is nothing new; traditionally it has inspired the work of metaphysicians and theologians. Since religious faith no longer appears capable of supporting our beliefs, Hutchins is all set to call on the Greek example.

> Now Greek thought was unified. It was unified by the study of first principles. Plato had a dialectic which was a method of exploring first principles. Aristotle made the knowledge of them into the science of metaphysics. Among the Greeks, then, metaphysics, rather than theology, is the ordering and proportioning discipline. . . . In metaphysics we are seeking the causes of the things that are. It is the highest science, the first science, and as first, universal. It considers being as being, both what it is and the attributes which belong to it as being.[17]

Hutchins may grant that other disciplines can study, in their own fashion, questions of the nature and purpose of human beings; what makes metaphysics more fundamental than all such inquiries, however, is that it bases the study of this nature and purpose on that of being, the ground of all things. What object of study does not participate in being? How could our understanding of being not affect our understanding of anything that is? For this reason, metaphysics qualifies as the most general and unifying science of all, and so the most essential to education.

Having strengthened his claim that metaphysics can reveal at the profoundest level both the aim of life and that of education, and therefore should constitute the central aim of education, Hutchins proceeds to deduce the proper order of a university curriculum directed to that aim.

> Metaphysics, the study of first principles, pervades the whole. Insep-arably connected with it is the most generalized understanding of the nature of the world and the nature of man. Dependent on this and subordinate to it are the social and natural sciences. In due subordination in the teaching of these we include historical and current empirical material. Such material ceases to be the whole of

these sciences as studied in a university and becomes instead an aid in understanding their principles. In a university like this it should be possible to get an education; it is possible to get one in no other way, for in no other way can the world of thought be presented as a comprehensible whole.[18]

The theory of education implied by this curriculum becomes clearer when we consider how, in such a university, we would study education. First of all, we would inquire into what education essentially is. Such a study would proceed from an account of the first principles and causes of being as such, from an account of what it means for anything that exists to have a reason for being. For example, we would consider whether a claim that there is a reason why justice exists involves a claim that justice contributes to some ultimate, constructive goal of the universe, or one that it was brought into existence by the universe's perfect creator, or some comparable first principle. This study would thus enjoin us to articulate the nature of education with the nature of humans and other things in the world, all viewed as having reasons for their being that are mutually consistent. We would learn how education fits into a harmonious, satisfying picture of everything that is, and from such knowledge we could deduce the proper end of education. At last we would be in a position to inquire about its means, and to evaluate and improve whatever means are currently in use with respect to how well they conduce to their proper end.

To be effective educators, then, we need the guidance of a prior theory of the aim of education, one which should be part of a larger, metaphysical theory of humanity, nature, and being. This is why educators have everything to learn from the questions and ideas of metaphysicians. This argument of Hutchins is echoed by Bloom, who followed Hutchins in advocating a "Great Books" and metaphysical approach to liberal education. Consider Bloom's explanation of where that education recently went wrong:

> The crisis of liberal education is a reflection of a crisis at the peaks of learning, an incoherence and incompatibility among the first principles with which we interpret the world, an intellectual crisis of the greatest magnitude, which constitutes the crisis of our civiliza-

tion. But perhaps it would be true to say that the crisis consists not so much in this incoherence but in our capacity to discuss or even recognize it. Liberal education flourished when it prepared the way for a discussion of a unified view of nature and man's place in it, which the best minds debated on the highest level. It decayed when what lay beyond it were only specialties, the premises of which do not lead to any such vision.[19]

How is it that we today have little capacity to recognize this crisis of first principles, this capitulation to an education in specialties? How is it that we no longer appreciate Hutchins's metaphysical philosophy of education? The blame or credit for this must largely go to Dewey.

Hutchins's theory of education relies on the possibility that we can study scientifically the first principles and causes of being—a possibility which Dewey denies. For Dewey, any genuine science must issue in results that contribute to the liberalization of our democratic society; this purpose gives science as a human enterprise its pragmatic value. Hutchins's metaphysics does not qualify as such a science because, Dewey contends, it would direct our education, and by extension our society, in an authoritarian, escapist, and irrational manner. It would restrict our capacity to criticize injustices in our schools and society, and it would protect those who want to keep things illiberal and undemocratic.

To make this case, Dewey considers what Hutchins's theory of education implies about "the inherent nature of knowledge and intelligence in relation to the locus of authority in matters intellectual."[20] He interprets Hutchins's position as follows.

I understand President Hutchins to hold that there is a power or faculty of Reason or Intellect . . . which is capable of grasping first and ultimate truths that are the measure and criterion of all inferior forms of knowledge, namely, those which have to do with empirical matters, in which knowledge of both the physical world and practical affairs is included. I understand him to hold that only on the basis of a hierarchical order determined on the basis of these truths could order be brought out of present disorder.[21]

According to this position, our reason essentially amounts to a capacity to grasp first and ultimate truths, metaphysical reasons for being; these truths constitute the locus of authority in intellectual matters because they function as the measure and criterion of all inferior, empirical and practical knowledge. If an object of the latter type of knowledge cannot be given a reason for being consistent with all the other first and ultimate truths, then presumably it should be disqualified as knowledge (or reformulated and fudged). Conversely, no empirical or practical knowledge may function as the measure and criterion of our metaphysical knowledge of these truths; no such knowledge could force us to abandon or revise these truths. It is this inequality in the functions of these two kinds of knowledge, this hierarchical order determined on the basis of metaphysical truths, that Dewey finds intellectually authoritarian.

But that is not all. Dewey finds that such a metaphysical locus of intellectual authority is likely to give aid and comfort to authoritarian forms of social order. The reason why is that it prevents us in principle from investigating whether empirical and practical facts, particularly entrenched political interests, may to some degree also determine our metaphysical beliefs. Until we subject these beliefs to this kind of scrutiny, we risk accepting beliefs that actually serve other, more worldly, antidemocratic interests. Indeed, when we look at societies that did not value this kind of critical investigation, such as those in which Greek philosophy and medieval theology flourished, we find flourishing alongside those speculative pursuits slavery and dogmatism. The principled insulation of first and ultimate truths from criticism except by other such truths appears to parallel the insulation of a social elite from criticism except by itself. Metaphysics, like religion, functions in such an uncritical environment like a political opiate.

> . . . The old metaphysical and theological philosophies reflected the social conditions in which they were formulated. By their translation into terms of reason, these conditions were given support.[22]

Is this going on in our society? What makes an investigation of this possibility worth pursuing is not only that it bears on the abstract status of metaphysical and theological philosophies, but especially that it promises to give us more vigilant control over our own social conditions, so that we may keep our society from lapsing into the authoritarian mores of those former times, and may promote society's growing liberalization. Thus our democracy stands to gain a lot from an empirical and practical inquiry into the political nature of our metaphysical beliefs, and to lose everything from the proscription of such inquiry by a metaphysical ideology, one that steers us away from these social concerns and toward escapist reverie. For this reason, it would be imprudent, irrational, to install metaphysics at the locus of authority in education.

Because metaphysical inquiry and ideas are liable to have socially as well as intellectually authoritarian consequences, because in the light of our democratic aspirations they appear escapist and irrational, Dewey finds them worthless as guides to the practice of education. They cannot compose a science of being, because they have no genuinely scientific, pragmatic value. He argues that we democratic liberals should seek guidance elsewhere; as an alternative to Hutchins's position, he posits:

> . . . the primary place of experience, experimental method, and integral connection with practice in determination of knowledge and the auxiliary role of what is termed Reason and Intellect in the classic tradition.[23]

What educators need to know in order to improve their practice is to be found in changing experience through adaptive experiment. Metaphysical ideas are useful only insofar as they contribute to the experimental process of gathering empirical knowledge that promises to help us cope better with problems we are experiencing (for example, by helping us form not final theories but theoretical hypotheses). On their own, they just do not count as knowledge.

Dewey criticizes Hutchins, then, for promoting a desire for metaphysics that is dangerously misleading. Dewey would presumably raise similar objections to the metaphysical sympathies of Bloom and Cavell. He would object to Bloom's two claims, in particular, by contending that once we understand what the consequences to our liberal democracy are of living by metaphysical ideals, we would not find the search for such ideals so desirable, nor would we want to foster that search in education. Hence any attempt to conceive of liberal education as a way of responding to metaphysical longing would be for him a mystification of the true desire for education, a desire rooted in what our society has learned by historical experience to value.

Is Dewey right? Is there another, nonmetaphysical way of understanding the invitation, the desire, that motivates liberal learning? Do liberal learners need to worry about being lovers—or only about being liberals? And is there another way of understanding constructively the metaphysical questions that occur to us, intimating that we stand related to some perfect reason for being?

In a move that initially begs the question in favor of Dewey, I am going to reformulate the first question above as: What if Dewey were right?—in order to explore what that would mean for liberal education. To do this, I shall examine the work of the contemporary philosopher who has pushed the antimetaphysical proclivities of Dewey's pragmatism furthest: Richard Rorty. Rorty sharpens Dewey's antimetaphysical arguments to the point where he has reason to indict Dewey himself, and other empiricists, of indulging their own dubious desire for metaphysics. At the same time, curiously enough, Rorty is prepared to agree with Cavell and Bloom that the animating spirit of liberal learning is eros. "General education—education that is not simply learning the tricks of the trade—is basically erotic."[24] These two trains of thought intersect in his review of *The Closing of the American Mind* when, like Bloom, he takes Socrates to be his educational hero, although for Deweyan reasons rather than the Platonic, metaphysical ones Bloom favors:

> What matters to us "intellectuals," as opposed to the [Bloomian] "philosopher," is the imaginativeness and openness of discourse, not proximity to something lying beyond discourse. Both Platonists and Deweyans take Socrates as their hero. For Plato, the life of Socrates did not make sense unless there was something like the Idea of the Good at the end of the dialectical road. For Dewey, the life of Socrates made sense as a symbol of a life of openness and curiosity. It was an experimental life—the sort of life that is encour-

aged by, and in turn encourages, the American democratic experiment.[25]

Explicating the arguments that lead to the vision of liberal education implicit in this passage will be the project of the next few chapters. It will hopefully become clear why liberal learners, according to Rorty, need no longer concern themselves with a thing's or event's essential, perfect reason for being; rather, they should profitably restrict their concern to how we may redescribe the accidental aspects of things and events in order to accomplish certain valued purposes. In keeping, then, with the hypothetical question: What if Dewey were right? Rorty may be read as furnishing us not with a conclusive refutation of the metaphysical liberal education of Hutchins, Bloom, and others, but simply with a demonstration that a Deweyan liberal education is a noncontradictory, viable alternative, one which, furthermore, possesses some distinct practical advantages.

Yet this latter conception of liberal education unavoidably broaches the all-too-familiar question of our time: Whose values? Who determines the purposes which a Deweyan liberal education is supposed pragmatically to serve? Rorty attempts to answer this question in a measured way by proposing the values of a democratic hero-figure, the liberal ironist. It is against the capacity of this figure to cope with the cultural antagonism stirred up by the above questions, and the longing this inspires, that I shall finally measure the potential of the moral perfectionist. I shall argue that Rorty's conception of the liberal learner, however useful, needs to be revised so as to address more seriously our metaphysical concerns. This argument will hopefully enable me to join Dewey's and Rorty's idea that liberal education should promote a pluralistic and democratic society with Hutchins's, Bloom's, and Cavell's idea that liberal education should be motivated by a quest for self-understanding carried out in conversation with others. It will hopefully enable me to conceive of a philosophy of liberal education that employs metaphysical questioning without the authoritarian baggage of metaphysical principles.

The rest of this book may be outlined as follows. In the second chapter, I examine Rorty's critique of metaphysics in education, of the idea that there is a perfect order of things on which our learning should be focused. Like Dewey, though with greater sophistication, Rorty argues that such an order of things would have to be grounded on some absolutely authoritative, indubitably certain, epistemological knowledge. He recounts how Enlightenment philosophers sought to establish the possibility of such knowledge; he examines how Descartes, to this end, equated the problems of reason and of personhood with that of consciousness, and how this equation was elaborated by Locke and Kant. Yet the idea of consciousness in this equation became more and more problematic, leading Nietzsche finally to explain why such knowledge was untenable, and to aver instead that our beliefs are really based only on assertions of our will to power. Such a realization challenges us to accept that there is no perfect order of things, and that the desire to find such an order is merely a resentful reaction against events that exceed our control. All possibility of metaphysical reassurance, it would appear, is destroyed, along with the Enlightenment idea that social conflict can be rationally resolved, and culture reformed in part through education.

Rorty argues, however, that, contrary to some of Nietzsche's conclusions, the latter idea can in fact survive the destruction of metaphysical reassurance. Indeed, he maintains that this destruction is not to be mourned, for out of it comes a keener appreciation of human potential, in particular, of what educated human reason and personhood are capable of achieving. In the third chapter, I explain how Rorty reformulates the Cartesian problem of reason in the light of Nietzsche's critique, so as to disjoin it from the problem of consciousness while distancing it from some of the more disturbing, nihilistic implications of Nietzsche's arguments. Using the work of Sellars, Quine, Davidson, Wittgenstein, and Dewey, Rorty develops a pragmatically historicist, conversational conception of reason more attuned to the hope for communal, cultural solidarity.

In a parallel fashion, I explain in the fourth chapter how Rorty reformulates the problem of personhood so as to disjoin it as well from the problem of consciousness, and to match it to his conversational conception of reason. He uses the work of Gadamer, Nietzsche,

Harold Bloom, Davidson, and Wittgenstein to construct a theory of how selves form themselves, thus developing a pragmatically historicist conception of personhood as edifying selfhood, attuned to the hope for individual distinction.

Conversational reason and edifying selfhood thus form the two principal aims of a Rortyan liberal education. The fifth chapter begins with an elucidation of how these aims lead Rorty, in response to Allan Bloom, to reenvision the idea of a Socratic education in an anti-Platonic, antimetaphysical key more appropriate to our democratic aspirations, thereby further reinforcing Dewey's criticism of Hutchins. Rorty dedicates such an education instead to exploring the resources for democratic reform in one's own and in other, contingent, historical cultures. His liberal education is explicitly and necessarily multiculturalist. This enables him to appreciate the role that eros or longing plays in liberal learning, without attaching that longing to any metaphysical object. The longing in liberal learning is, rather, that for an opportunity where you can use various cultural resources for conversational edification to struggle heroically with a problem in your culture.

My response to this conception of liberal education proceeds from a consideration of how Rorty would cope with conflicts between the two aims of his education. His approach to this problem is expressed by the figure of the liberal ironist, one who affirms both her or his solidarity with a culture and her or his project to distinguish herself or himself individually, and who attempts to prevent these commitments from disrupting each other by compromising between them in practice, rather than Platonically reconciling them in theory. This compromise takes the form of applying to her or his life a distinction between the private and public realms, one rooted in liberalism. I am troubled, however, by the fact that, because there is no naturally correct way to make such a distinction, we can apply it only in controversial ways that are bound to produce cultural antagonism. Rorty's liberal ironist, who is invested in this distinction, thus appears helpless to stop her or his interactions with others from turning into, as Laclau and Mouffe have compellingly described, a perpetual struggle between hegemonic polities, where the question, *Whose values?* is forever raised by ever-new cultures in conflict.

Although I admire the way Laclau and Mouffe have stressed the tensions between different cultures, rather than those between "the public" and "the private," I do not see why such cultures can only coexist in a democracy through an acceptance of antagonism and a readiness to take advantage of it. Chapter Six, then, attempts to save the gains of Rorty's conceptions of conversational reason and of edifying selfhood from the problems of his pragmatic liberalism by showing how these conceptions may be modified to help us disarm any such state of conflict. It detaches the conceptions from Rorty's liberalism, and attaches them instead to a version of moral perfectionism drawn from Cavell. It explores how we may initiate youth into a pacifistic culture suited to a culturally diverse world by engaging them in a practice of conversational edification that stresses aporetic questioning. Such a questioning joins youth and adulthood in an acknowledgment of our mortal vulnerability and in an affirmation of the joy of being alive. Given our current conjuncture, characterized by doubts about liberalism, I suggest that a commitment to the disarming politics of such a conversation in education—unlike other forms of political action—may distinguish what moral perfectionism has to offer as a project of cultural reform. Correspondingly, I define the edification of the moral perfectionist as the realization that you question, you long, to be true to the mystery you are, more than the persona you may redescribe yourself as; this realization stands to offer a more fulfilling conception of our selfhood. Morally perfectionist conversational edification, I believe, will enable us to put liberal learning in the service of cultural reform for a multicultural democracy. It offers us a promising philosophy of liberal education.

2

THE PROBLEM WITH METAPHYSICS: THE EPISTEMOLOGY OF RESENTMENT

What if Dewey were right? Before we can respond directly to this question, we will need to repair some conspicuous flaws in Dewey's criticism of Hutchins. As we saw in the last chapter, Dewey challenged Hutchins's call to make metaphysics the focus of liberal education because metaphysics implies a hierarchical order of knowledge that conflicts with democratic values. At the time, I took this to be a plausible objection, yet now I need to consider an obvious riposte to Dewey: namely, so much the worse for democratic values. Hutchins could reply that, "authoritarian" or not, the structure of knowledge implied by metaphysical inquiry is true, and either our democratic values would have to be made consistent with that knowledge, or they would have to be rejected as false, however desirable. Hutchins himself, as all his writings show, was supremely confident that the value of democracy could be established on metaphysical grounds. Should we not seek, then, to put our democratic values, and our liberal education, in conformity with such truths, instead of closing our eyes because they appear threatening? Perhaps we do need to be more vigilant about the way metaphysical inquiry has been used to protect social elites from criticism; yet does it follow from such abuses—like the abuses of other sciences—that metaphysics cannot still be the star of liberal education?

Another flaw is that, in other writings, Dewey did recognize the need for metaphysical inquiry. Although he consistently fought against Greek metaphysics and its idealist tradition, in his later work, *Experience and Nature*, he saw that this fight required the formulation of an alternative metaphysics, one which limned the "generic traits of experience" in terms of "empirical naturalism."[1] What Dewey did not appear to see is that this project concedes a crucial point to Hutchins: namely, that "if you have a different opinion [about human nature and the aim of education], you must show that you have a better metaphysics."[2] The Dewey who grounds our pragmatic endeavors not only in experience but in the first principles of empirical naturalism, therefore, is in no position to criticize Hutchins for promoting the role of "Reason and Intellect in the classic tradition."

But these flaws may lie in Dewey's limitations as a thinker, and not in the pragmatist critique of metaphysics which he helped initiate. Indeed, I have found that Rorty, one of Dewey's leading successors, pursues the critique in a more rigorous and thoroughgoing fashion. Like Dewey, he takes aim at what metaphysics implies about "the inherent nature of knowledge and intelligence in relation to the locus of authority in matters intellectual." He does not so much dispute particular metaphysical claims to truth—for example, that there exists an idea of the perfect Good which is absolutely separate from all physical things and events we would call "good"—so much as he attacks the whole notion of there being fundamental, "first and ultimate truths that are the measure and criterion of all inferior forms of knowledge." His target is, thus, not metaphysics *per se*, much less any particular metaphysics, but the fact that any metaphysics requires an epistemology. He argues that, even if the idea of epistemology were not authoritarian and antidemocratic, it would be incoherent. Metaphysics, then, loses its claim to truth, and collapses into an unverifiable tale we tell ourselves, perhaps to put our political discontents to sleep.

This chapter will elucidate the reasoning behind Rorty's critical interpretation of the history of epistemology from Descartes to Nietzsche. I shall explain why the search for epistemological knowledge arose and then foundered, and how that failure ultimately led Nietzsche to demystify the desire for metaphysical ideals. Rorty's account shows that a substantial part of philosophical history is on Dewey's side against Hutchins.

In his central book, *Philosophy and the Mirror of Nature,* Rorty studies how epistemological concerns and inquiries grew out of the Western project to make knowledge the foundation of culture, to reform culture rationally.[3] This project presumed we could identify that body of knowledge, those "first and ultimate truths," which constitute the natural criteria for establishing what else is true and valid in our culture. Hutchins's view of the role of metaphysics in education is clearly a continuation of this project. Both Hutchins and his predecessors suppose that such fundamental truths are the special province of philosophers, and they define accordingly the philosopher's vocation as one of sitting in a tribunal that judges the state of our culture's rationality.

> Philosophers usually think of their discipline as one which discusses perennial, eternal problems—problems which arise as soon as one reflects. . . . Philosophy as a discipline thus sees itself as the attempt to underwrite or debunk claims to knowledge made by science, morality, art, or religion. It purports to do this on the basis of its special understanding of the nature of knowledge and of mind. Philosophy can be foundational in respect to the rest of culture because culture is the assemblage of claims to knowledge, and it finds these foundations in a study of man-as-knower, of the "mental processes" or the "activity of representation" which make knowledge possible. To know is to represent accurately what is outside the mind; so to understand the possibility and nature of knowledge is to understand the way in which the mind is able to construct such representations. Philosophy's central concern is to be a general theory of representation, a theory which will divide culture up into the areas which represent reality well, those which represent it less well, and those which do not represent it at all (despite their pretense of doing so).[4]

This key passage sets out themes we will be returning to repeatedly; for the present, it observes that epistemology is at the center of the philosopher's vocation because it leads philosophers to the knowledge that they need—and that the rest of us need to learn from them—in order to criticize our culture accurately and to reform it rationally. Philosophers in general, and metaphysicians in particular, understand their discipline to be concerned with solving fundamental and ahistorical problems. The most fundamental and ahistorical—the most philosophical—part of philosophy is that body of knowledge about the nature of knowledge and knowing: epistemology. By virtue of their epistemology, philosophers will be able to know that their knowledge of the solutions to their problems, metaphysical and otherwise, is truly knowledge; in other words, that they truly know that these are the right solutions. Indeed, once philosophers have established an adequate epistemology, they will have the philosophical means to verify the truth of what nonphilosophers claim to know as well, that is, of all the claims to knowledge that make up our culture. They will be in a position to determine where our culture is built on true claims and where on false, which cultural aspirations are rationally well founded and deserve our support, and which are not and ought to be resisted. In sum, the philosopher's vocation is to educate us in a special, epistemological knowledge of the nature of knowledge and knowing, epistemological knowledge both informed by and supportive of metaphysical knowledge of general human nature, so that we may become more reasonable cultural reformers.

Where does this idea that a philosophical education for cultural reform depends on epistemology come from? Rorty locates its origins in the history of the Enlightenment. He concentrates on three elementary notions that compose it.

> We owe the notion of a "theory of knowledge" based on an understanding of "mental processes" to the seventeenth century, and especially to Locke. We owe the notion of "the mind" as a separate entity in which processes occur to the same period, and especially to Descartes. We owe the notion of philosophy as a tribunal of pure reason, upholding or denying the claims of the rest of culture, to the eighteenth century and especially to Kant, but this Kantian notion presupposed general assent to Lockean notions of mental processes and Cartesian notions of mental substance. In the nineteenth century, the notion of philosophy as a foundational discipline which "grounds" knowledge-claims was consolidated in the writings of the neo-Kantians. Occasional protests against this conception of culture as in need of "grounding" and against the pretensions of a theory

of knowledge to perform this task (in, for example, Nietzsche and William James) went largely unheard.[5]

Putting things a bit differently, we can reconstruct the history of this idea backwards through the answers to three key questions. First: Why did philosophers assume that they had a calling to critically enlighten us about the grounds on which our culture stands? Answer: because Kant had demonstrated to them, in his three *Critiques*, that philosophy may be understood as a tribunal which seeks to establish the *a priori*, fundamental criteria for judging whether the claims of science, morality, and art are true. Philosophers accomplished this when they secured knowledge of what may legitimately, rationally count as knowledge in these three spheres of culture, that is, when they secured epistemological knowledge of the essence of cultural knowledge. This answer raises a second question: Why did Kant and his followers assume that the essence of cultural knowledge was knowable? Answer: because Locke had demonstrated to them, in his *Essay on Human Understanding*, that we could inquire into the nature of knowledge in general and arrive at a theory of knowledge that explains how we acquire any cultural knowledge. According to this theory, impressions of the external, material world are received by our immaterial minds through the senses; given these impressions, we can then strive to know through reflection how accurately they represent the world. Although Kant, in the *Critique of Pure Reason*, criticized important elements of the theory, he formulated his own theory of knowledge based on Locke's two key components: sense-impressions, or what he called "intuitions," on the one hand, and ideas, or what he called "concepts," on the other. Finally, this answer raises a third question: Why did Locke and his followers assume that a theory of knowledge must explain how an immaterial mind interacts with a material object? Answer: because Descartes had proved to them, in his *Meditations*, that we know the existence of the mind prior to, and better than, the existence of the body, a proof which entails that mind and matter are distinct substances. He admitted, however, in reply to critical inquiries from Princess Elizabeth, that this dualistic ontology poses a problem for how mind and body communicate, a problem that Locke aimed to solve with his theory.

Descartes, Locke, Kant, and the Enlightenment thinkers they influenced, then, arrived at a conception of a philosophical education in culture composed of three notions: the notion of mind, the notion of a theory of knowledge, and the notion of philosophy as a tribunal of pure reason. Yet as Rorty notes, Nietzsche, among others, eventually protested against this conception. The reasons for this are rooted in problems that emerged with these notions, problems that Nietzsche's three predecessors failed to solve. Proceeding from those problems, Nietzsche provided us with a devastating critique of epistemology, and so of the belief in metaphysical ideals. The desire to believe in such untenable ideals, he asserts, is a resentful evasion of the challenge to live creatively.

Rorty proceeds to trace these three notions back to three problems which the above philosophers took to be interlocked; each of these notions was formulated by them in successive attempts to respond to these problems. He begins by examining the notion of the mind. This notion was arrived at by Descartes after he had equated the problem of personhood and the problem of reason with the problem of consciousness. Rorty defines the first problem as follows:

> Let us call the "problem of personhood" that of what more a human being is than flesh. This problem has one form in the pre-philosophical craving for immortality, and another in the Kantian and romantic assertion of human dignity—but both cravings are quite distinct from problems about consciousness and about knowledge. Both are ways of expressing our claim to be something quite different from the beasts that perish.[6]

This problem concerns the metaphysical question—to which Rorty will return later: What gives human life and death meaning? Related to this problem, and partly a response to it, is the second problem of reason, which, inherited from ancient philosophy, concerns the speculative questions, What is knowledge? and, How does our capacity to know, our reason, our soul, distinguish human beings from mortal animals? Now it is a measure of Descartes's originality that he grasped how both of these central problems could be addressed methodically by reducing them to the more scientifically tractable problem of consciousness. The latter concerns questions about the causal relations between states of awareness, bodily states, and states of the world outside the body. Rorty details the difference between these three problems as follows:

> [The problem of reason] . . . takes different forms in Aristotle's hylo-morphic account of knowing, Spinoza's rationalistic account, and Kant's transcendental account. But these issues are distinct both from those about the interrelations between two sorts of things (one spatial and the other nonspatial) and from issues concerning immortality and moral dignity. The problem of consciousness centers around the brain, raw feels, and bodily motions. The problem of reason centers around the topics of knowledge, language, and intelligence—all our "higher powers." The problem of personhood centers around attributions of freedom and of moral responsibility.[7]

By reformulating the two latter problems as aspects of the former, Descartes can claim that we will at last be able to understand what it means to be essentially a spiritual and rational being, by understanding what it means to be conscious. The key to the riddle of our immortality and reason turns out, then, to be the workings of the mind.

Now Rorty charges that Descartes's equation of these distinct problems was a crucial mistake, that his account of what it means to have a mind cannot even begin to solve all of these problems. Rorty's argument for this has two parts. The first part remarks that the Cartesian notion of the mind, which proceeds from the problem of consciousness, cannot be derived from the notion of the soul, which belongs to the problem of reason, and thus has no relevance to the latter problem. Admittedly, Greek, Medieval, and Renaissance philosophers all tended to identify the soul with our capacity to contemplate and acquire knowledge of universal ideas; this would seem to lend credibility to the idea that, since the Cartesian notion of the mind resembles the above notion of the soul, the Cartesian problem of consciousness must be analytically derivable from the Greek problem of reason. Yet Rorty reconstructs a history of the concepts available to Aristotle and to Descartes that refutes such an idea. He summarizes his findings as follows.

> The notion of the "separation between mind and body" means different things, and is proved by different philosophical arguments, before and after Descartes. The hylomorphic [Aristotelian] epistemology which thought of grasping universals as instancing in one's intellect what the frog instanced in its flesh was, thanks to the rise of mathematical physics, being replaced by a law-event framework which explained froghood as possibly a merely "nominal" essence. So the notion of reason as a faculty of grasping universals was not available for use in a premise proving the distinctness of the mind from the body. The notion which would define what could "have a distinct existence from the body" was one which would draw a line between the cramps in one's stomach and the associated feeling in one's mind.
>
> I have suggested that the only criterion which will draw this line is indubitability—that closeness to the Inner Eye which permits Descartes to say (in a sentence which would have astonished . . . antiquity) that "nothing is easier for the mind to know than itself."[8]

Between the Aristotelian notion of the soul and the Cartesian notion of the mind intervened Copernican astronomy and Galilean physics, which cast doubt on the Aristotelian claim to grasp the truth of universals through contemplation alone. Since Descartes subscribed to these new mathematical and mechanical sciences, he could not rely on this Aristotelian claim to establish either that human beings and animals, or that mind and body, are essentially distinct. Now, to secure the latter distinction, he did have recourse to the indubitability of the Cogito, but this new claim cannot uphold the idea that the soul is capable of contemplating universals, or that human beings, unlike animals, are essentially soul. The first part of Rorty's argument, then, demonstrates that the Cartesian notion of the mind cannot be derived from the Aristotelian notion of the soul, so that Descartes's formulation of and concentration on the problem of consciousness, centered on indubitability as the mark of the mental, leaves the Greek problem of reason unaddressed.

Rorty next considers whether the Cartesian problem of consciousness can be derived from the problem of personhood. He constructs a thought-experiment involving an imaginary race which inhabits the other side of the galaxy. The Antipodeans, as he calls them, live in ways nearly identical to our own; they differ from us in only one significant aspect: they lack any notion of a mind.

These beings did not know that they had minds. They had notions like "wanting to" and "believing that" and "feeling terrible" and "feeling marvellous." But they had no notion that these signified *mental* states—states of a peculiar and distinct sort—quite different from "sitting down," "having a cold," and "being sexually aroused."[9]

Mindless, Antipodean science was free to impress the culture at large with feats that we can barely conceive of:

Neurology and biochemistry had been the first disciplines in which technological breakthroughs had been achieved, and a large part of the conversation of these people concerned the state of their nerves. When their infants veered toward hot stoves, mothers cried out, "He'll stimulate his C-fibers." When people were given clever visual illusions to look at, they said, "How odd! It makes neuronic bundle G–14 quiver, but when I look at it from the side I can see that it's not a red rectangle at all." Their knowledge of physiology was such that each well-formed sentence in the language which anybody bothered to form could easily be correlated with a readily identifiable neural state. This state occurred whenever someone uttered, or was tempted to utter, or heard the sentence. This state also sometimes occurred in solitude and people reported such occasions with remarks like "I was suddenly in state S–296, so I put out the milk bottles." Sometimes they would say things like "It looked like an elephant, but then it struck me that elephants don't occur on this continent, so I realized that it must be a mastodon." But they would also sometimes say, in just the same circumstances, things like "I had G–412 together with F–11, but then I had S–147, so I realized that it must be a mastodon." They thought of mastodons and milk bottles as objects of beliefs and desires, and as causing certain neural processes. They viewed these neural processes as interacting causally with beliefs and desires—in just the same way as the mastodons and milk bottles did.[10]

What we have in the Antipodeans, then, is a race without a notion of mind, but with a sophisticated science of physiology which has put its stamp on their everyday language and become approved common sense. The Antipodeans are convinced that they partake of the same nature as other material entities, so they are troubled by no problem of consciousness. Instead, they are able to build out of their material interactions with their world a causal, scientific language for describing and predicting (but not necessarily for commanding, justifying, emotionally or stylistically expressing, and so on) their behavior.

Now Rorty broaches the second part of his argument against the Cartesian equation of the three problems by asking: Must the Antipodean's lack of a notion of mind, and their substitute language of "neural processes," alter their ability to make sense of their own personhood?

To answer this question, Rorty imagines that the race is visited by a contingent of Terran philosophers who want to know whether or not the Antipodeans, regardless of what they think, *really* have minds. Rorty's thought-experiment accordingly consists of putting to the Antipodeans questions designed to elicit evidence as to whether they experience what we would dub "mental states." These questions converge on the basic issue of whether they have indubitable, "incorrigible knowledge of raw feels." By raw feels, Rorty means sensations that defy adequate verbalization, like the pang that a piece of music gives you, or what sadness feels like before you know the word "sadness"; for you to have incorrigible knowledge of raw feels means that when you report that you have such sensations, no one else can claim to know better that you do not have them. Unfortunately, though, the Antipodeans have no way of grasping what these philosophers are driving at, for they can only understand what they, and anybody else, experience in their brains in terms of scientifically corrigible knowledge that certain neural states have occurred. Indeed, the more the Terrans interrogate them, the more they begin to suspect that we Terrans are incorrigibly deluded about our so-called mental states, and that such states *really* correspond only to very imperfectly known neural states.

After sketching some rather comical exchanges between these two parties, Rorty draws the moral that neither can make its reductive rejection of the other's account of thinking rationally stick. Both should instead acknowledge that the apparent disjunction between "incorrigible knowledge of raw feels" and "corrigible knowledge of neural states" boils down merely to a *difference* between whole vocabularies which nevertheless enable their speakers to say and do the *same* things. "No predictive or explanatory or descriptive power would be lost if we had spoken Antipodean all our lives."[11] Hence nothing turns, in the end, on whether we determine that the Antipodeans do or do not really have minds; we may dispense with this question as academic.

From this thought-experiment we may draw two conclusions. First, that, like the Antipodeans, we did not have to postulate a split between mind and body in order to talk about traditionally "mental" phenomena like believing, willing, thinking, and so on, let alone to talk about other forms of experience. This means that, second, there is no reason why our notion of personhood must depend on a notion of mind, even if historically it happens that we have learned to associate them. Nothing in principle prevents us from distinguishing ourselves from other beings in other terms that, nevertheless, entail all the same practical consequences as our current mental terms. In sum, Rorty's account of the Cartesian notion of the mind demonstrates that this notion, while designed to address the problem of consciousness, is irrelevant not only to the problem of reason but also to the problem of personhood; nothing follows for these last two problems from what it means to have a mind.

But of course, most Enlightenment philosophers happened to follow Descartes—toward Nietzschean nihilism. Once on that fateful path, they soon realized that the notion of mind split off from matter only partially solved the problem of what it means to be conscious; it left unanswered the question of how the mind interacts with the material world to produce a consciousness *of* objects. Furthermore, since they assumed, with Descartes, that the problems of personhood and reason could be equated with the problem of consciousness, they sought for a solution to the mind-body gap that would reveal something essential about our reason and personhood.

It was for this purpose that Locke proposed his theory of knowledge, the second of the three notions that compose our conception of epistemological education for cultural reform. The theory attempted to explain consciousness as a matter of "the possibility or extent of accurate representation which is the concern of a discipline called 'epistemology'."[12] Consciousness is thus linked to our reason via our capacity to acquire knowledge. And in order to understand how consciousness works—which, as Descartes suggested, should illuminate how our reason works and how we are elevated above animals—we need to develop a consistent theory of whether and how it is possible that our mental ideas represent the material world, and of the degree to which our current ideas do this accurately.

According to Rorty, however, the Lockean notion of a theory of knowledge confused explanation with justification. This becomes apparent when we consider two different paradigmatic challenges to any claim to knowledge, one coming from the skeptic proper to the Greek problem of reason, the other from the skeptic proper to the Cartesian problem of consciousness. Rorty notes that the former, Pyrrhonian skeptic typically worried about whether it is possible to arrive at verifiable truths without reasoning in a circle or dogmatically. To answer her or him, we need to get a clear idea of how we may methodically deduce truths from self-evident premises (the obscure but suggestive model for such a method usually being the geometric proof). In contrast, the Cartesian skeptic was troubled by "the problem of getting from inner space to outer space—the 'problem of the external world' which became paradigmatic for modern philosophy."[13] To answer this "veil-of-ideas" skepticism, we do not need knowledge so much of what counts as a deduction of truths, as of what counts as an accurate representation, knowledge which could then be applied to evaluate the fit between a particular idea and the bit of the world it purports to represent.

Locke in effect thought that you could rebut these two skeptics together. As the pioneer of the epistemological discipline that would provide us with knowledge of how the mind represents the world, he ventured to *explain* how certain mechanical functions of the mind and sense-organs cause ideas to represent the world, so that we may know if our ideas are accurate by verifying that our minds and senses are functioning properly. As an inheritor of Descartes's work, and specifically of the equation of the problem of consciousness with that of reason, however, he also assumed that this explanation would *justify* certain beliefs, that it would answer the Greek skeptic as well, by demonstrating that certain ideas about the world, acquired in the proper manner under standard circumstances, are self-evidently true, and may serve as premises for deducing other truths. This led to the confusion T.H. Green called:

> . . . the fundamental confusion, on which all empirical psychology rests, between two essentially distinct questions—one metaphysical, What is the simplest element of knowledge? the other physiological, What are the conditions in the individual human organism in virtue of which it becomes a vehicle of knowledge?[14]

Why did Locke mix these up? Why did he think that an account of what caused or regularly causes one to have a belief could serve to justify that belief? The answer, in Rorty's story, is that Locke followed Aristotle in holding that "knowledge of" an object must be prior to "knowledge that" such-and-such a proposition about that object is true. When we accept this premise, it makes sense that if we want to account for our "knowledge that," we must first of all understand how "knowledge of" is possible. Locke explained "knowledge of" by postulating a "faculty of understanding" on which, like a wax tablet, objects made impressions. The moment we receive these impressions, we have immediate knowledge of the objects; the impressions are not considered, then, merely one type of causal antecedent among others to knowing that a certain proposition about the objects is true (others being, for example, the prevailing rules of inquiry in one's culture, one's kicking a stone, one's class background, and so forth). With this notion of impression, though, Locke departs from the Aristotelian notion of "knowledge of," and runs right into the problem of how to account for our knowledge of—these impressions.

> It is as if the *tabula rasa* were perpetually under the gaze of the unblinking Eye of the mind—nothing, as Descartes said, being nearer to the mind than itself. If the metaphor is unpacked in this way, however, it becomes obvious that the imprinting [of impressions] is of less interest than the observation of the imprint—all the knowledge gets done, so to speak, by the Eye which observes the imprinted tablet, rather than by the tablet itself. . . . Whereas Aristotle had not to worry about an Eye of the Mind, believing knowledge to be the *identity* of the mind with the object known, Locke did not have this alternative available. Since for him impressions were *representations*, he needed a faculty which was *aware* of the

representations, a faculty which *judged* the representations rather than merely *had* them—judged that they existed, or that they were reliable, or that they had such-and-such relations to other representations. But he had no room for one, for to postulate such a faculty would have intruded a ghost into the quasi-machine whose operation he had hoped to describe. He kept just enough of Aristotle to retain the idea of knowledge as consisting of something object-like entering the soul, but not enough to avoid either skeptical problems about the accuracy of representations or Kantian questions about the difference between intuitions with and without the "I think."[15]

Locke repeats here the Cartesian mistake of thinking that the Greek idea of the soul can be preserved in the modern idea of the mind. In order to explain mechanistically how we are able to know that our representations are accurate, he had to assume the Aristotelian premise that "knowledge of" is prior to "knowledge that." Unfortunately, because he was dealing with a Cartesian notion of the mind, rather than with an Aristotelian notion of the soul, this premise landed him in the following dilemma. Either he had to accept that "knowledge of" objects entails an infinite regress of impressions of impressions, which defies explanation. Or he had to revise his earlier assumption and accept the priority of some act of "knowing that," which raises the problem of justifying our beliefs (against Greek skepticism) all over again.

Therefore we must hold that Locke's theory of knowledge is inadequate, because its explanation of how we acquire knowledge cannot justify why we should take such knowledge, including the theory's own knowledge-claims, to be true. His theory can neither account for our consciousness nor for our reason or personhood. Indeed, the theory's confusions of explanation and justification, "knowledge of" and "knowledge that," appear almost predictable once the theory is premised on the Cartesian equation of the three problems.

This criticism of Locke was in large measure—minus the examination of Locke's Aristotelian and Cartesian inheritance—affirmed by Kant. Indeed, Kant's transcendental turn represented an attempt to steer clear of the Lockean impasse by substituting for the notion of impression, and for its matching, passive, *tabula rasa* notion of the mind, a notion of synthesis and of an actively "constitutive" mind. The mind became a judging as well as a receiving faculty; it judiciously synthesizes the sensible intuitions it receives with the proper, innate, *a priori* concepts of the understanding in order to constitute representational knowledge of the world, or "synthetic" truths, on the one hand, and knowledge of instances of logical laws, or "analytic" truths, on the other. Unlike Locke, then, Kant accepted the necessity for a primordial act of "knowing that"; this implies a mind that transcends the order of empirically knowable and mechanically causal objects and processes, so as to constitute that order from a distance as *consciousness of* that order. By acknowledging the above necessity, then, Kant actually emancipates us, our minds, reason, and personhood, from Locke's mechanically determinist universe.

Like Locke, though, he also assumed that the Cartesian problem of consciousness demanded, and set the terms for, an epistemology that could answer skepticism, specifically of the veil-of-ideas variety. To the problem of knowing whether our representations of things are accurate, and therefore whether our beliefs about those things are true, Kant replied that we could know this by showing how the mind constitutes such representations in accordance with "rational principles of pure understanding." Furthermore, this actively constitutive mind could serve as a signal metaphor for philosophy itself. Just as the individual's conscious mind transcends and organizes its representations rationally, philosophy could preside over our society's cultural representations as a tribunal of pure reason, the third notion central to the philosophical education for cultural reform we have been exploring.

Oddly enough, however, something like Newton's law of force holds here: for this transcending action of the subject, there is an equal and opposite reaction of the absolutely receding thing-in-itself. This made Kantian transcendence a Trojan horse for Cartesian skepticism. The mind of the transcendental subject can only experience the thing-for-him, the objects of his consciousness; the objects in themselves, as they (really) are prior to their (distorting) representation, remain out of reach. Kant himself, confident that he could demonstrate *a priori* that our consciousness works rationally, would leave no room for the parenthetical qualms above. However, since his transcendental account of our experience required an irreducible distinction between the thing-for-us and the thing-in-itself, most of his successors saw in this requirement the smuggling in of the possibility of radical error. Once we posit the thing-in-itself out of reach of our knowledge, we cannot know that things-in-themselves really exist, and have no sure reason, therefore, to suppose that they do. All that are left are things-for-us, which confine us to the interior of Cartesian consciousness, unable to penetrate the veil of ideas and represent the things in the world truly. The problem of reason again remains unaddressed by this account of our consciousness.

The stage was set for Nietzsche to push these epistemological antinomies to their final, destructive conclusion. Although Rorty does not examine in detail Nietzsche's role in the history of epistemology, Rorty's later writings, especially *Contingency, Irony, and Solidarity*, clearly harvest the ground that Nietzsche has tilled. I propose, therefore, to complete Rorty's historical account of epistemology by explaining how the intractable difficulties in the Cartesian equation of the problems of personhood, reason, and consciousness led Nietzsche to formulate a new, daring conception of personhood, one which allowed him to dispense with the ideas of reason and consciousness altogether.

Nietzsche responded to the Kantian dilemma with the argument that if there are only things-for-us, then we ought to worry less about the "thing" part of the formula, and cultivate instead the "for us" side. The former worry, chewing over questions like: How can we know things-in-themselves? How can we get past Cartesian skepticism? and ultimately: How can we ground our culture on true knowledge? appears unresolvable. Yet we may be able to simply shrug it off if we consider what more lies in store for us when we realize that the world is constituted by our own mental acts. Such a realization extends to us, to our will, the power to create and control our world, a power that could overshadow any of the blessings of epistemological certainty. Nietzsche remarks in his notebooks, edited under the title *The Will to Power*, that:

. . . what things "in-themselves" may be like, apart from our sense receptivity and the activity of our understanding, must be rebutted with the question: How could we know that things exist. "Thingness" was first created by us. The question is whether there could not be many other ways of creating such an apparent world—and whether this creating, logicizing, adapting, falsifying is not itself the best-guaranteed reality; in short, whether that which "posits things" is not the sole reality; and whether the "effect of the external world upon us" is not also only the result of such active subjects—The other "entities" act upon us; our adapted apparent world is an adaptation and overpowering of their actions; a kind of defensive measure. The subject alone is demonstrable; hypothesis that only subjects exist—that "object" is only a kind of effect produced by a subject upon a subject—a *modus* of *the subject*.[16]

Following Kant, Nietzsche takes things to be products of a subject's mental acts. He proceeds to question, however, the nature of these acts, whether they must be characterized as ones of knowing rather than ones of adapting, falsifying, and so on. Now such a question could have set him on an epistemological chase for knowledge to ground his claims to be knowing a thing, rather than, say, falsely imagining it. Yet in the wake of Kant's troubles, the question instead suggests to him that the more important issue is not what the "true nature" of the act is, but *that one acts*, and that everything we experience depends on those acts, whatever (we deem) their nature. In one stroke, he liberates himself from epistemological entanglements by affirming the central power of the subject who posits the things of her or his world. Indeed, eliminating the last vestiges of "thingness" on which epistemology could hang its hat, Nietzsche decides—as if by fiat—that the act is not one of "positing" at all, with all the investigative connotations that the term carries, but rather one of "adapting to and overpowering" other actions that the subject is reacting to, that is, one of dominating a world made up of actions in a way that creates the features of one's own world.

To develop this ontology of actions, Nietzsche redescribes the subject of such acts, so that it is no longer related primarily to objects of consciousness. He needs to do this, because a subject's actions would otherwise still be ruled by a prior perception or knowledge of the world; they could not from the first dominate or create one's world. Nietzsche's remarks above about the effects produced by a subject upon a subject, then, become more comprehensible when we follow him in substituting for the Kantian, conscious subject a notion of the subject as a center of force. This move allows him to bracket off and ignore both the problem of consciousness, of how things may appear to us, and the problem of reason, of how things may appear truly or falsely.

> Every center of force adopts a perspective toward the entire remainder, i.e., its own particular valuation, mode of action, and mode of resistance. The "apparent world," therefore, is reduced to a specific action on the world, emanating from a center.
> Now there is no other mode of action whatever; and the "world" is only a word for the totality of these actions. Reality consists precisely in this particular action and reaction of every individual part toward the whole—
> No shadow of a right remains to speak here of *appearance*—[17]

In place of a world that appears to conscious subjects, Nietzsche advances a world that each of its parts, its subjects, act on. Thus everything, including what used to be called merely "objects," becomes a subject in potential conflict with other subjects. Each subject is the agent of an action (even if, as in the case of a stalactite, a comparatively leisured one), and each is the center of a world composed of the active causes and effects of that action. That world and its central subject, however, can always be subsumed under more powerful actions that install another hegemonic subject at the center of a larger world; each subject is also subjected to the actions of others. This means that, in place of the apparent objects in the world that define that world, Nietzsche also advances a subject's central action, and the reactions of other subjects which it provokes and copes with, that delimit the world from that subject's perspective. To determine one's world, then—rather than to become conscious of it—one needs to "transform the belief 'it *is* thus and thus' into the will 'it *shall become* thus and thus' ": the boundaries of one's world are secured not by the comparative truth of one's beliefs, but by the comparative power of one's will.[18] Thus, in place of "truth" and "appearance," finally, we would do better to account for our subjective experience in terms of "my will to power," on the one hand, and "another's conflicting will to power," on the other. These terms recognize that we are the creative centers of our world, and its partisan defenders against the equally egocentric attempts of others to dominate it. Thus the will to power becomes for Nietzsche the mark of our personhood.

This alternative account of our personhood, departing from Kant's subject of consciousness to let loose that subject from its epistemological vacillations, brings us to Nietzsche's critique of metaphysical ideals as resentful perversions of the will to power (a brilliant twist on Augustine's definition of evil as perversion of the will). Once we admit that we project and assert the meanings of things and events in the world, that things and events do not have their own independent reasons for being, any Platonic desire to orient ourselves to a perfect reason for being, to understand and live by metaphysical ideals, would only confuse and weaken our will to power. Such an eros would make us think that these ideals are things-in-themselves to be known, an assumption that this successor of Descartes, Locke, and Kant has demonstrated is problematic and dispensable.

Furthermore, by indulging a desire for metaphysical ideals, we would prevent ourselves from realizing that every ideal dialectically implies a deidealization of some part of our experience. Thus we would fail to take responsibility for, and control over, the devaluing of a part of our physical world. Instead of acting out of a will to power, we could find ourselves in the predicament of reacting, unconsciously, to the actions of a stronger, hegemonic subject by resentfully accepting a world not our own.

> But have you ever asked yourselves sufficiently how much the erection of *every* ideal on earth has cost? How much reality has had to be misunderstood and slandered, how many lies have had to be sanctified, how many consciences disturbed, how much "God" sacrificed every time? If a temple is to be erected *a temple must be destroyed*: that is the law—let anyone who can, show me a case in which it is not fulfilled![19]

Not only are our ideals not things-in-themselves to discover, but they are historical inventions, "temples," built on a foundation of antithetically "low," "undesirable" aspects of life that we have debased. Moreover, we cannot justify this *act* of debasement on the grounds that it is "fair" to the world as it ought to be, or "true" to the world as it is, for there could be no *vision* of a higher, moral and true, ideal world unless we have already presumed that part of the world, the "sinful" or "deceptive" part, the part which stimulates in us desires that we *fear*, "deserves" to be actively suppressed. As with Kantian transcendence, for every act of valuing there is an equal and opposite act of devaluing. Thus shadowing metaphysics, or what Nietzsche calls our "ascetic ideals," like the true, the good, and the beautiful, is our curse against those desires and springs of life—caused by other centers of force—we unhappily could not master, a curse motivated by the spirit of *"ressentiment"* or resentment. Yet if we could free ourselves from this impulse to idealize and curse what we are afraid is beyond us, from this idle and childish, unconscious *ressentiment*, we would be in a better position to coopt those forces by transforming them into our *own* will to power, however finite and mortal. Against the worship of metaphysical idols at the expense of the rest of our world, Nietzsche summons us to aestheticize our love of life in *all* its physical forms. In a comparable fashion, Freud will later encourage us to sublimate rather than repress our libidinal desires.

Nietzsche's account of metaphysical eros as *ressentiment* needing to be aesthetically transformed leads to two conclusions. First, it argues for the historicist point that there are no natural, universal ideals of perfection, but only acts of valuing performed by different people in a variety of circumstances. Hence there are no neutral criteria—no criteria that are not themselves already partisan acts of valuing—by which we may judge which values are truer or better than others. Second, it furthermore argues that even after we have accepted a particular scheme of values—perhaps calling it an ideal order of things—that scheme may always be interpreted as a scheme of devaluations: our "highest values" equal our "harshest devaluations." This point, to which we shall return later, became a cornerstone of Walter Benjamin's critique of historical progress: "There is no document of civilization which is not at the same time a document of barbarism."[20] Any affirmation of values invites conflict from adherents to rival values, a conflict that cannot be resolved by appealing to some natural standard—hence a conflict resolvable only by triumphant force.

So much, then, for the notion that erotic desire could lead to an understanding of perfection, or that tragedy could provoke us to seek a more meaningful reason for being. So much for Hutchins's dream of a metaphysical liberal education grounded on "first and ultimate truths." Without a plausible epistemology to support metaphysical beliefs, those beliefs begin to seem like the rhetorical mystifications that Dewey suspected them to be. Unlike Dewey, though, Nietzsche does not think that any knowledge-claims, including empirical ones, can avoid serving the interests of a will to power. Characteristically, he takes accepting without nostalgia the loss of the dream that there is heaven beyond the world of power struggles to be a test of strength.

> It is a measure of the degree of strength of will to what extent one can do without meaning in things, to what extent one can endure to live in a meaningless world *because one organizes a small portion of it oneself.*[21]

Yet it is doubtful whether, at the end of Nietzsche's critique of epistemology and metaphysics, there is anything left but the spirit of destruction. Although Nietzsche calls on us to create and organize our own worlds, he appears to demand that we live only by the rule of whim. Are there to be no guides for the will? Is everything permitted? Is all external constraint to be considered simply an enemy will, fit only to be resisted and overpowered? Under such conditions, is it possible to create a culture that can be commonly affirmed? With these questions, which threaten any conception of social order, we begin to appreciate the cost of his renunciation of the problem of reason, a renunciation that makes him, in the eyes of many, the prophet of nihilism, or at least of the quintessentially postmodern question: Whose values?

Rorty believes that Nietzsche's critique need not lead to destructive chaos, however. But to avoid this, his critique needs to be revised in some important ways. In particular, it needs to address more constructively the utopian hopes we have traditionally placed in reason, and the individual hopes placed in a more meaningful idea of personhood. In the next three chapters, I shall explore how Rorty recasts Nietzsche's critique in the language of key contemporary philosophers in order to make it serve the purposes of educationally promoting a liberal, multicultural democracy. As a prelude to this discussion, I would like to return to Kant's epistemology, for Rorty points out an opportunity to leave its path of reasoning which promises to steer clear of, in a different way than Nietzsche does, the thing-in-itself *cul de sac*.

Rorty remarks that: "With Kant, the attempt to formulate a 'theory of knowledge' advanced half of the way toward a conception of knowledge as fundamentally 'knowing that' rather than 'knowing of'—halfway toward a conception of knowing which was *not* modelled on perception."[22] Rorty faults him for not going all the way, however, and explains his shortcoming as due to a "confusion between predication (saying something about an object) and synthesis (putting representations together in inner space)."[23] According to Kant, there could be no object to predicate properties of without a prior act of synthesis; synthesis, therefore, is a causal antecedent to predication. But does it justify the predication; does it constitute a reason for predicating truth, for instance, of certain sentences, as in "I know that 'sentence p' is true"? Kant, like Locke, tries to explain how certain peculiar, in this case "transcendental" events *cause* a claim about knowledge to be rationally *justified*. In Locke's case, this explanatory account proved incoherent. In Kant's case, it appears, bereft of Lockean confusions, unnecessary.

> For [Kant's] notion that our freedom depends on an idealistic episte-
> mology—that to see ourselves as "rising above mechanism" we have
> to go transcendental and claim to have "constituted" atoms and the
> void ourselves—is just Locke's mistake all over again. It is to assume
> that the logical space of giving reasons—of justifying our utterances
> and our other actions—needs to stand in some special relationship
> to the logical space of causal explanation so as to insure either an
> accord between the two (Locke) or the inability of the one to interfere
> with the other (Kant). Kant was right in thinking accord was senseless

and interference impossible, but wrong in thinking that establishing
the latter point required the notion of the "constitution" of nature
by the knowing subject.[24]

This passage raises the following key questions. How else might we
establish that an accord between "the logical space of giving reasons"
and "the logical space of causal explanation" is senseless, and that
any interference between these two spaces is impossible? Would
such an alternative, non-Kantian argument for these points still
manage to address the problem of what it means to know something,
the problem of reason? How about the problems of consciousness
and personhood? Lastly, would the alternative permit us to save the
gains of Nietzsche's critique of epistemology and metaphysics, while
avoiding its incitements to value conflict, in both senses of the
phrase?

These questions usher us out of Rorty's history of Cartesian epistemology and into his speculations on what a post-Cartesian, postmod-
ernist philosophical education for cultural reform can properly accomplish, and how the promise of that accomplishment is bound
to the desire for a liberal education. Before we proceed to explore
these new lines of thought, though, let me summarize how the
preceding arguments have reinforced Dewey's point against Hutchins, that metaphysical inquiry is necessarily based on a structure of
knowledge which is untenable.

Rorty points out, in effect, that Hutchins's idea that we need
metaphysical inquiry to establish a realm of "first principles" separate
from and prior to empirical knowledge proceeds from a neo-Kantian
picture of philosophy and culture, one where philosophical, epistemological knowledge is supposed to ground our cultural beliefs
and to guide cultural reform. He recounts how this picture was
historically composed of the notions of mind, of the theory of knowledge, and of philosophy as a tribunal of pure reason, and how
Descartes, Locke, and Kant fit these notions together as they attempted to equate the problem of consciousness with that of reason
and that of personhood. Rorty casts doubt, however, on whether
this equation ultimately makes sense, and so on whether the three
notions can form a coherent picture of what we need to learn in

order to make culture rational. His arguments shed light on why Nietzsche then attempted to dispense with the problems of reason and of consciousness in favor of a conception of personhood focused on the will to power, and how this conception led Nietzsche in turn to criticize the desire for metaphysical ideals as a shrinking away from that will out of the spirit of fearful resentment. Unfortunately, this critique appears to destroy the possibility of cultural reason. Yet Rorty holds out the hope that a revision of the critique may disclose a way to leap out of both the frying pan of Cartesian epistemology supporting the claims of metaphysicians like Hutchins, and Nietzsche's nihilistic fire.

In the next two chapters, we will explore how Rorty undoes the bonds formed by the Cartesian equation of the three problems; in the fifth chapter, we will consider whether his maneuvers also free us from the tendency in Nietzsche's conception of the will to power to provoke antagonism. We shall start by focusing on the tension between justification and explanation, examining how this tension may be dispelled by letting reason and consciousness be apples and oranges.

3

FROM EPISTEMOLOGY TO CONVERSATION

The previous chapter concluded with the question of whether it is possible to separate the logical spaces of causal explanation and of rational justification without having to reach for the Kantian double-edged sword of transcendental consciousness. This question in effect challenges us to demonstrate how we may both explain what causes us to believe certain things, and argue that those beliefs are justified, without either confusing these two actions, *à la* Locke, or, like Kant, subsuming them to some prior action that transcendentally constitutes our consciousness of objects. The latter transcendental action theoretically accomplishes this, as we mentioned, by synthesizing in the mind sensible intuitions and concepts of the understanding; the distinction between these two elements is then reflected in the two kinds of truths produced by this synthesis: synthetic and analytic truths. Now Rorty takes up this challenge and argues that we can perform both of the former actions independently of any act of mental synthesis, that, indeed, the very notion of such a mental synthesis is incoherent. This argument will more generally try to establish that we may eliminate the tension between explanation and justification in cultural knowledge by separating the problem of reason from that of consciousness.

For the most part, Rorty presents his case by summarily alluding to pioneering works of recent analytical philosophy, and by incisively intervening in the debates they provoked so as to interpret their significance in the direction of his antiepistemological point. Since it is likely that many readers will be less familiar with these specialized articles than with the previously discussed classics of Enlightenment thought, I shall reconstruct and spell out Rorty's argument by examining the articles in a more expansive fashion.

The argument draws on the work of Wilfrid Sellars, W.V.O. Quine, and Donald Davidson to sharpen a point made earlier by Ludwig Wittgenstein and Dewey: namely, that we can translate our talk about true knowledge in culture more usefully into talk about forms of linguistically holistic behavior, and about what practical differences such forms could make to how we purposefully respond to specific situations. It attacks the Kantian notion of mental synthesis, and the equation of reason and consciousness which this notion consolidates, in roughly four steps. The first is to recount how the hard distinction between intuitions and concepts was blurred by Sellars's critique of the Myth of the Given. The second step is to recount how the matching distinction between synthetic and analytic truths was likewise blurred by Quine's critique of analyticity. The third step is to claim that although these critiques undermine the Kantian equation of reason with consciousness, they can nevertheless support an alternative notion of reason, one modeled after Davidson's theory of truth in a language which aims to render perspicuous useful options for reweaving our web of beliefs, in other words, for speaking coherently. Finally, the fourth step is to draw the implications of Davidson's theory for how we should go about justifying our beliefs. We may bring these implications into focus by pursuing the example set by Wittgenstein and Dewey, philosophers who aspired therapeutically to dissolve needlessly distractive antinomies, while raising larger questions about our most practical needs. One of those antinomies, it turns out, is the problem of consciousness; one of the needs which this antinomy downplayed is that for ethical conversation and solidarity.

The first step in the argument proceeds from a celebrated essay of Sellars entitled "Empiricism and the Philosophy of Mind."[1] Here, Sellars criticizes various versions of "the Myth of the Given": the idea that our empirical knowledge, which he tacitly assumes is the core of our cultural knowledge, must be grounded on some noninferential, immediate, infallible "knowledge of" what is simply there or given (for instance, knowledge of "a green sense-datum" or of "my thinking"). This idea entails that confusion and error arise only when we depart from this elementary knowledge to elaborate reflectively on it. Rather than reconstructing Sellars's full argument against this idea, I shall just block out the two main points that Rorty takes away from it.

One of these points is that we should retire the old saw that empirical knowledge is based on what is immediately given to experience. Sellars begins to argue for this by recalling that a familiar version of the Myth of the Given is:

> . . . the idea that there is, indeed *must be*, a structure of matter of fact such that (a) each fact can not only be non-inferentially known to be the case, but presupposes no other knowledge either of particular matter of fact, or of general truths; and (b) such that the noninferential knowledge of facts belonging to this structure constitutes the ultimate court of appeals for all factual claims—particular and general—about the world.[2]

Historical examples of such a privileged structure of fact include the Lockean realm of "impressions" and the Kantian of "sensible intuitions"; these realms theoretically furnish us with the raw, fundamental data which we afterwards assemble into a true and coherent picture of the world via "reflection," "mental synthesis," "cognition," or some corresponding process.

Sellars questions what gives any conceivable *report* of such data its authority or credibility. He finds that for anyone, including the reporter, to credit a report like "this is green" with expressing authoritative knowledge of the presence of a green object (say, a green mirage), that person must *also* know that the verbal (or in another instance, quasi-verbal) token "this is green" is a reliable symptom of a green object's presence. To think, therefore, that in Sellars's characteristically precise words, "observation 'strictly and properly so-called' is constituted by certain self-authenticating nonverbal episodes, the authority of which is transmitted to verbal and quasi-verbal performances when these performances are made 'in conformity with the semantical rules of the language'," is to get things backwards; we rather start with a comprehensive knowledge of how to speak a language—which we share with other speakers—and then transmit the social authority invested in this linguistic know-how in rule-governed ways to certain "observational episodes."[3] This means that, while we may allow that some event (a), where you see a green object under such-and-such circumstances (or have your visual receptors and nervous system stimulated in a particular way, or however the event equivalent to these is formulated), is a necessary, perhaps even sufficient, *cause* of another event (b), where you utter "this is green," we cannot take (a) alone to *justify* you in granting the utterance the authority of a true observational report, in *knowing* that there is a green object present. Such knowledge would depend on, among other things, knowledge of the synchronic structure of the language that you use diachronically to make the report, a structure that cannot be reduced itself to any specific event that can be reported. Even if we do not want to label this linguistic knowledge innate or nonempirical, and would prefer to consider it a type of empirical knowledge or know-how that you accumulate through various ostensive lessons, the upshot here is that your empirical knowledge that "this is green" can only be grounded on—other empirical knowledge.

> One could not have observational knowledge of *any* fact unless one knew many *other* things as well. . . . For the point is . . . that observational knowledge of any particular fact, e.g. that this is green, presupposes that one knows general facts of the form X *is a reliable symptom of* Y. And to admit this requires an abandonment of the traditional empiricist idea that observational knowledge "stands on its own feet." Indeed, the suggestion would be anathema to traditional empiricists for the obvious reason that by making observational knowledge *presuppose* knowledge of general facts of the form X *is a reliable symptom of* Y, it runs counter to the idea that we come to know general facts of this form only *after* we have come to know by observation a number of particular facts which support the hypothesis that X is a symptom of Y.[4]

Does this argument, that empirical knowledge cannot be founded on raw observational reports, not to mention the immediate experiences reported, entail that empirical knowledge is groundless? Sellars thinks not; he contends rather that "the metaphor of 'foundation' is misleading in that it keeps us from seeing that if there is a logical dimension in which other empirical propositions rest on observational reports, there is another logical dimension in which the latter rest on the former."[5] How these two dimensions *mutually support* each other articulates the other point important to Rorty: that empirical knowledge is *holistic*.

Sellars embarks on a demonstration of this holism by wondering how an observational episode like the one just discussed, or any other "inner episode" (for example, having a toothache, having a brainstorm, and so forth) can "combine *privacy*, in that each of us has privileged access to his own, with *intersubjectivity*, in that each of us can, in principle, know about the other's."[6] He ventures to explain how this is possible by weaving an allegorical myth. Imagine that our prehistoric ancestors once could only talk about their actions in a language whose vocabulary could only describe the public properties of objects locatable in physical space and time. Except for this vocabulary difference, this behaviorist language had a logical and expressive power comparable to our own. Proceeding from this premise, then, he considers the following questions. First: "What resources would have to be added to the . . . language of these talking animals in order that they might come to recognize each other and themselves as animals that *think*, *observe*, and have *feelings* and *sensations*, as we use these terms?" And second: "How could the addition of these resources be construed as reasonable?"[7]

To answer these questions, Sellars brings onto the stage a revolutionary psychologist named Jones. When Jones examines the varieties of intelligent behavior in his society, he reasons as follows:

> Suppose now, that in the attempt to account for the fact that his fellow men behave intelligently not only when their conduct is threaded on a string of overt verbal episodes—that is to say, as *we* would put it, when they "think out loud"—but also when no detectable verbal output is present, Jones develops a *theory* according to which overt utterances are but the culmination of a process which begins with certain inner episodes. *And let us suppose that his model for these episodes* which initiate the events which culminate in overt verbal behavior *is that of overt verbal behavior itself. In other words,*

> *using the language of the model, the theory is to the effect that overt verbal behavior is the culmination of a process which begins with "inner speech."*[8]

Jones thus hypothesizes a prior domain of unobserved, nonempirical, inner verbal-like behavior to explain how both observed, intelligent verbal behavior and observed, intelligent nonverbal behavior are possible. The inner episodes—what we would call thoughts—differ from the overt episodes after which they are modeled not metaphysically, in substance, but methodologically: the latter are established by empirical observation, the former by theoretical postulation. Hence "these [inner] episodes are 'in' language-using animals as molecular impacts are 'in' gases, not as 'ghosts' are in 'machines'."[9] It may turn out, Jones might speculate, that at some time in the future (for instance, after his people have left Earth to colonize the planet Antipodes) these inner episodes will be able in turn to be explained empirically (for instance, by using the vocabulary of neural events). But for now, however incomplete, the theory needs no such backup in order to start to make intelligent behavior more comprehensible.

Pursuing this train of thought, Jones next attempts to extend his notion that there are inner analogs to overt verbal behavior to explain the behavior of perceiving something. Just as we often credit someone with perceiving a green object when that person reports, "There is a green object," Jones reasons that you may also perceive a green object when there is silently "in" you an "inner report" of a green object. *"Seeing that something is the case* is an inner episode in the Jonesean theory which has as its model *reporting on [its] looking that something is the case."*[10] As with his theory of intelligent behavior, he wants the inner report to be by definition prior to any overt report; he thus registers this priority by calling the inner episode not a (willed) report but an (automatic) impression of an object. His theory of perception "postulates a class of inner—theoretical—episodes which he calls, say, impressions, and which are the end results of the impingement of physical objects and processes on various parts of the body."[11]

Skipping over the subtleties of this theory, which Sellars painstakingly unfolds, we come to the myth's denouement.

> Let us suppose that as his final service to mankind before he vanishes without a trace, Jones teaches his theory of perception to his fellows. . . . They begin by using the language of impressions to draw theoretical conclusions from appropriate premises. (Notice that the evidence for theoretical statements in the language of impressions will include such introspectible inner episodes as *its looking to one as though there were a red and triangular physical object over there*, as well as overt behavior.) Finally he succeeds in training them to make a *reporting* use of this language. He trains them, that is, to say "I have the impression of a red triangle" when, and only when, according to the theory, they are indeed having the impression of a red triangle.[12]

We can imagine that each of Jones's students begins to learn how to use the language of impressions by observing the behavior of another, say Smith, and reporting, when evidently appropriate, "Smith is having the impression of a red triangle," whereupon Jones either applauds or criticizes the student's performance. Later, the student would learn how to observe his own behavior in this regard, and to report, still under Jones's supervision, "I have the impression of a red triangle." Finally, the student would become so fluent at this language that he would no longer need either Jones's supervision or even any conscious effort to make first-person reports, though when he compares his third-person reports to the first-person reports of others, he may still feel less than cocksure about his knowledge of another's impressions. At this point, we can imagine that he might be struck by his "privileged access" to his own impressions. And when his society in effect ratifies this privilege, making it a convention of all speakers that first-person reports of impressions are to be accepted as incorrigible, then *we* may say that Jones's impressions have become full-fledged mental entities, in our sense of the term.

Sellars draws from this denouement the following moral:

> The myth helps us to understand that concepts pertaining to certain inner episodes—in this case *impressions*—can be primarily and essentially *inter-subjective*, without being resolvable into overt behav-

> ioral symptoms, and that the reporting role of these concepts, their role in introspection, the fact that each of us has a privileged access to his impressions, constitutes a dimension of these concepts which is built on and presupposes their role in intersubjective discourse. It also makes clear why the "privacy" of these episodes is not the "absolute privacy" of the traditional puzzles. For . . . the fact that overt behavior is evidence for these episodes is built into the very logic of these concepts as the fact that the observable behavior of gases is evidence for molecular episodes is built into the very logic of molecule talk.[13]

This moral regarding impressions may be evidently extended to other types of inner episodes, such as thoughts, desires, regrets, and so on. The story about Jones and his society, then, demonstrates that the concepts we use to characterize all such episodes must combine privacy with intersubjectivity, because these concepts can only make sense in a language that we pick up and use in public contexts. It answers Sellars's two questions about how we may reasonably translate a behaviorist language into a mentalist one, by introducing a race of behaviorists to a new theory which postulates a class of "mental" events, modeled after already-describable physical events, in order to explain puzzling forms of overt behavior. In so teaching them the jargon of this theory, moreover, we Jonesian mentalists learn that these mental events need not differ in substance from their physical analogs. Although the concepts of mind and body have distinct functions in the theory of behavior, the difference between them is not a first principle of a prior metaphysical ontology, but was rather created and countenanced for the purposes of pursuing this particular explanatory methodology.

We can now connect the moral of this allegory to Sellars's previous point that empirical knowledge is not founded on immediate experience, but rather each bit of it presupposes some other bit of empirical knowledge (that, for example, x is a token of y). It had then seemed that such knowledge must therefore be groundless, but the account of how Jones arrived at his theory of perception makes the whole idea that knowledge should be grounded in something no longer very plausible or useful. For this account demonstrates how we may either, like Jones, derive the existence and nature of impressions, construed as automatic quasi-reports, from that of empirical propositions, or, like traditional empiricists, derive the existence and nature of empirical propositions from that of impressions. Which one is "given," and serves to "ground" the other, depends on the entire language we and our community speak, whether its tokens are organized, for example, on behavioristic or mentalistic premises. Yet if that is the case, then our manifest ability to switch back and forth between these languages at will suggests that the decision to speak one or the other is finally ours to make, and is not determined by anything simply given (already in one of these languages). So to insist that, for empirical knowledge to be possible, one of these languages must be the right one, and that one of these "structures of matter of fact" must be pregiven, is to obscure the actual dependence of any such facts on the holistic logic of its language—which is *optional*. There are no natural atoms of knowledge, nor are there any naturally primal events of knowing, for whether x is a token of y or z is a matter of contingent, changeable convention.

We may, accordingly, come to recognize, as did Rorty, that the reason we got tangled up with mythical terms like "impressions" and "sensible intuitions" in the first place is that we assumed that there had to be some such atoms and events, which we needed to discover and describe. Interestingly enough, Dewey fell prey to the same assumption when he stressed, as we saw in the first chapter, "the primary place of experience . . . in determination of knowledge"—and then developed this stress into a metaphysics of empirical naturalism. Rorty points out, in the essay "Dewey's Metaphysics," that this Enlightenment assumption ironically led Dewey to substitute empiricist first principles for idealist ones.[14] Sellars enables us to see, then, that both Hutchins and Dewey run into problems as soon as they insist on epistemologically identifying what the primary determinants of knowledge must be. Sellars disabuses us of the need for such stipulations.

> The essential point is that in characterizing an episode or a state as that of *knowing*, we are not giving an empirical description of that episode or state; we are placing it in the logical space of reasons, of justifying and being able to justify what one says.[15]

Sellars's arguments thus fortify Rorty's criticism, discussed in the previous chapter, of the Lockean and Kantian attempt to make an explanation of how we acquire knowledge do duty for a justification of that knowledge. Sellars and Rorty advise us that, for the purposes of the latter enterprise, we would do well to worry less about the former types of explanation—including that which explains knowing as a mental synthesis of intuitions and concepts—and turn, rather, to consider how the "logical space of reasons" works. How, that is, we justify our beliefs holistically.

A similar critique of the Myth of the Given was propounded by Quine in his classic "Two Dogmas of Empiricism."[16] The second dogma at which he took aim was reductionism: "the belief that each meaningful statement is equivalent to some logical construct upon terms which refer to immediate experience."[17] Like Sellars (though in less detail), he argued that we just cannot formulate the kind of sense-data language that this dogma demands. Also like Sellars, he concludes that our cultural knowledge does not rest on immediate experience, but constitutes a "field of force" that, as a whole, exerts pressure on each claim to truth we make, old and new, to keep it coherently in line with the others.

Before we examine these converging conclusions, however, let us walk through Quine's treatment of the first dogma of empiricism, which corresponds to the second step in Rorty's argument. This dogma is bound to the Myth of the Given by the positivist verification theory of meaning, a theory that holds that we should understand the meaning of a statement to be the method by which we empirically confirm or infirm it. Quine remarks that "as long as it is taken to be significant in general to speak of the confirmation and infirmation of a statement, it seems significant to speak also of a limiting kind of statement which is vacuously confirmed, *ipso facto*, come what may; and such a statement is analytic."[18] Now, if there really are such analytic statements, which are distinct from synthetic statements that demand to be confirmed by something extralinguistic, then it may appear plausible that we need to explain how we are capable of churning out these two kinds of statements—an explanation furnished by the notion of mental synthesis. Indeed, this first dogma,

too, has Kantian origins: it consists of the belief that analytic statements exist, and of the idea of analyticity which such statements
presuppose:

> Kant conceived of an analytic statement as one that attributed to its
> [grammatical] subject no more than is already conceptually con-
> tained in the subject. This formulation has two shortcomings: it
> limits itself to statements of subject-predicate form, and it appeals
> to a notion of containment which is left at the metaphorical level.
> But Kant's intent, evident more from the use he makes of the notion
> of analyticity than from this definition of it, can be restated thus:
> a statement is analytic when it it true by virtue of meanings and
> independently of fact.[19]

Quine is not sure that this idea of analyticity makes sense. He
observes that there are two classes of true statements conventionally
deemed analytic. The first comprises those statements which are
logically, but trivially, true; they remain true even when we systematically reinterpret their semantic components, provided we fix our
interpretation of their logical particles (for instance, "not," "and,"
"or," "if," "then," and so forth). His example of such a statement
is: "No unmarried man is married." The second class comprises
those nontrivial statements which can be turned into logically true
statements by substituting synonyms for certain of its components.
His example here is: "No bachelor is married," where we can replace
"bachelor" with its synonym "unmarried man" in order to get the
previous logically true statement. Now the question that initially
troubles Quine is: Since the second, more significant class of analytic
statements apparently relies on some notion of synonymy, how
should we understand this notion?

Quine tries out several approaches to this question. First, he
attempts to derive synonymy, and hence analyticity, from a prior
notion of meaning. He soon concludes, however, that:

> since the theory of meaning is sharply separated from the theory of
> reference [by the difference between the intension and extension of
> a term], it is a short step to recognizing as the primary business of
> the theory of meaning simply the synonymy of linguistic forms and
> the analyticity of statements; meanings themselves, as obscure inter-
> mediary entities, may well be abandoned.[20]

In other words, a theory of meaning just means a theory of intensional synonymy and analyticity; the latter is thus not something to be derived from the former. Next, he attempts to base synonymy on how terms are defined. But definitions do not grow on trees, they are formulated by lexicographers who empirically report on observed synonyms, thereby taking some general framework of synonyms, and notion of synonymy, for granted. The act of defining a term, therefore, cannot serve to determine how we originally understand synonymy. Finally, he attempts to get at synonymy through a notion of interchangeability. "A natural suggestion, deserving close examination, is that the synonymy of two linguistic forms consists simply in their interchangeability in all contexts without change of truth value—interchangeability, in Leibniz's phrase, *salva veritate*."[21] Chasing down this suggestion, however, he runs into the question of whether there might be multiword linguistic forms that are interchangeable *salva veritate*, and so, according to the formula, synonymous, but which are, in lexicographical fact, heteronymous. He finds that the sole way to rule out interchangeable heteronymous expressions is, once again, to assume a notion of analyticity which would distinguish intensional agreement from extensional; otherwise, if we confined interchangeability to a language where there were only extensional agreements between predicates, there would be "no assurance here that the extensional agreement of 'bachelor' and 'unmarried man' rests on meaning rather than merely on accidental matters of fact, as does the extensional agreement of 'creature with a heart' and 'creature with kidneys'."[22] So, although the notion of interchangeability does set noncircular conditions for synonymy, it depends on an advance understanding of analyticity—which synonymy was going to explain.

This last dead end leads Quine to give up the attempt to get a bead on analyticity by flushing out the essence of synonymy, and to try instead to tackle analyticity by explicitly constructing, in some artificial language, made-to-order "semantical rules." Here again, though, he ends up running into brick walls. Either we try to stipulate a semantical rule for generating analytic statements in an artificial language *L*—whereupon we produce rules that contain the mystery word "analytic." Or we try to dodge this circularity by first stipulating a semantical rule for generating a certain class of true statements, and only subsequently defining analyticity as follows: a statement is analytic if and only if it is true by virtue of this semantical rule. Whereupon we appeal not to an unexplained term "analytic" but to an unexplained phrase "semantical rule"; for "no one signalization of a subclass of the truths of L is intrinsically more a semantical rule than another; and if 'analytic' means 'true by semantical rules', no one truth of L is analytic to the exclusion of another."[23]

At this point, Quine concludes that we should "just stop tugging at our bootstraps altogether."[24] We have found no way to formulate what "analytic statement" or "analyticity" means, in nontrivial cases, that does not presuppose either these notions or equally problematical notions like "synonymy" or "semantical rules." For this reason, he finally condemns the whole lot of these notions, and the strict divide between analytic and synthetic statements.

> It is obvious that truth in general depends on both language and extralinguistic fact. The statement "Brutus killed Caesar" would be false if the world had been different in certain ways, but it would also be false if the word "killed" happened rather to have the sense of "begat." Thus one is tempted to suppose in general that the truth of a statement is somehow analyzable into a linguistic and a factual component. Given this supposition, it next seems reasonable that in some statements the factual component should be null; and these are the analytic statements. But for all its a priori reasonableness, a boundary between analytic and synthetic statements simply has not been drawn. That there is such a distinction to be drawn at all is an unempirical dogma of empiricists, a metaphysical article of faith.[25]

By exposing the pitfalls in what ought to be the straightest roads to a definition of analyticity, Quine transforms this truism into a dubious presumption. He effectively casts doubt as well on the idea that we need a corresponding notion of mental synthesis to account for how we are wired to generate the two types of true statements, since he has shown that these types cannot really be unequivocally distinguished from each other.

In their critiques of the two dogmas of empiricism, then, Sellars and Quine make the Kantian scheme to separate a causal explanation of our beliefs from a rational justification of them, by means of a transcendental act that synthesizes in the mind intuitions and concepts, look like a Rube Goldberg contraption. When Sellars attacks the dogma that empirical knowledge must be founded on a realm of immediately given experience, he renders problematic both the existence of a distinct realm of sensible intuition, and the need to postulate an act that synthesizes that realm with that of concepts of the understanding in order to produce empirical knowledge. When Quine attacks the dogma that we can know purely analytic, nontrivial, nonempirical truths, he renders problematic both the distinction between such truths and synthetic, empirical truths, and the need to postulate an act that would sort out our knowledge accordingly. Both of these thinkers furthermore conclude that our cultural claims to knowledge do not need to be grounded at all; they suggest that it ought to suffice for all human purposes if we justify our beliefs holistically, satisfying ourselves that each belief supports and is supported by every other belief we hold in a coherent system. Such a holistic approach should finally disentangle justification from explanation, and allow us to address the problem of reason, as well as to determine the causes of our beliefs, without involving ourselves in the problem of consciousness and its epistemological complications.

For Sellars, the holism of our cultural knowledge becomes apparent when we illuminate the "logical space of reasons" that justifies our beliefs. Quine, for his part, conceives of this logical space as "total science," and likens it to a "field of force whose boundary conditions are experience."[26] He unfolds this figure as follows:

> If this view is right, it is misleading to speak of the empirical content of an individual statement—especially if it is a statement at all remote from the experiential periphery of the field. Furthermore it becomes folly to seek a boundary between synthetic statements, which hold contingently on experience, and analytic statements, which hold come what may. Any statement can be held come what may, if we make drastic enough adjustments elsewhere in the system. Even a statement very close to the periphery can be held true in the face of recalcitrant experience by pleading hallucination or by amending certain statements of the kind called logical laws. Conversely, by the same token, no statement is immune to revision. Revision even of the logical law of the excluded middle has been

proposed as a means of simplifying quantum mechanics; and what difference is there in principle between such a shift and the shift whereby Kepler superseded Ptolemy, or Einstein Newton, or Darwin Aristotle?[27]

In this scheme of things, we do not get knowledge by logically verifying that statements are true to their empirical content; instead we get knowledge by adjusting, when deemed necessary, the whole network of our beliefs and meanings, our language, to experiences we undergo, to "sensory promptings."[28] The knowledge we claim, the statements we make, are the behavioral effects of specific events in the world and in our nervous systems; in this sense, the utterance of a statement depends on what caused it to be uttered. For all that, however, the statement's truth, goodness, or beauty—the degree to which we judge it to possess these qualities—does *not* depend on how accurately it represents some object or event, even its cause. We judge a statement, rather, on how easily it goes with other statements we regularly make, as well as on how effectively it enables us, identifiably and linguistically committed to certain beliefs and meanings, to cope with the events that prompted it. Thus, while a statement's utterance is bound to antecedent stimuli, its truth, its claim to knowledge (as well as its other claims), can only be evaluated with respect to how the speaker implicitly uses the entire language in which the statement is made. We can put this point in another way that spells out its departure from Kantian epistemology: "the logical space of causal explanation" and "the logical space of giving reasons" form "parallel planes," yet we do not need to appeal to some constitutive act of a transcendental subject to keep them apart, for what separates them is the simple difference between a specific act of moving your mouth and the potentially infinite implications of what you are saying.

If we accept this picture, however, then we may wonder whether it is still useful to call such knowledge-claims "empirical," as Sellars and Quine do. Quine (unlike Sellars) tries to address this question in his essay by elaborating the notion that statements may be closer to or further from the "experiential periphery of the field." He explains that a statement's distance from the periphery is roughly a function of how likely we are to revise it in the event of anomalous experience, in order to accommodate our field as a whole to that experience. Some statements, such as when one utters "water" while pointing to a body of water, and after having undergone a sensory experience of water, are likely to command the nearly universal assent of a particular, in this case English-speaking, language community. If a member of that community were confronted with an unusually disturbed body of water, she or he would probably hold the ostensive utterance "water" steady, and experiment with revising other conventional statements in her or his language such as "water is disturbed only when the gods are angry," statements which, being less directly prompted by a particular sensory experience, are less likely to command universal assent. This process of revision suggests that, although it is no longer viable to talk about the empirical content of an individual statement, we can still talk usefully, for the purposes of scientific description and prediction, about a loose division between observational statements which are less likely to be revised because their causes are more closely bound to sensory experience, and theoretical statements which are more likely to be revised because their causes are further from such experience. To call our knowledge empirical and to call oneself an empiricist, as Quine does,[29] is to claim that when we are confronted with anomalous experience, our most pragmatic course of action is to complicate our observational statements and simplify our theoretical ones.

Other philosophers, however, notably Davidson, have detected in the distinction between observational and theoretical statements the traces of yet another dogma. In his essay "On the Very Idea of a Conceptual Scheme,"[30] Davidson remarks that Quine, after disposing of the distinction between analytic and synthetic truths, nevertheless continues to derive from the experiential periphery of the linguistic field a general notion of "empirical content":

> The dualism of the synthetic and the analytic is a dualism of sentences some of which are true (or false) both because of what they mean and because of their empirical content, while others are true (or false) by virtue of meaning alone, having no empirical content. If we give up the dualism, we abandon the conception of meaning

that goes with it, but we do not have to abandon the idea of empirical content: we can hold, if we want, that all sentences have empirical content. Empirical content is in turn explained by reference to the facts, the world, experience, sensation, the totality of sensory stimuli, or something similar.[31]

Davidson distinguishes this idea of empirical content from Quine's idea of a "conceptual scheme," as evinced in statements like, "I continue to think of the conceptual scheme of science as a tool, ultimately, for predicting future experience in the light of past experience."[32] It appears, accordingly, that a conceptual scheme is something that one uses to do something to the content of experience. In this sense, both our observational and theoretical statements would be elements of our scientific conceptual scheme, but they would differ in their distance from the points where the conceptual scheme is affected by the content of experience. The distinction between observational and theoretical statements, then, rests on a larger distinction between empirical content and conceptual scheme—a dualism to which Davidson objects:

> I want to urge that this second dualism of scheme and content, of organizing system and something waiting to be organized, cannot be made intelligible and defensible. It is itself a dogma of empiricism, the third dogma. The third and perhaps the last, for if we give it up it is not clear that there is anything distinctive left to call empiricism.[33]

As we shall see, Davidson's critique of this third dogma furnishes Rorty with the key, third argumentative step he needs to exit from the epistemological tradition of philosophical education for cultural reform. Not only does the critique consolidate the separation, opened up by Sellars and Quine, of justification from explanation and the problem of reason from the problem of consciousness, but it broaches a constructive way to address the former problem while dumping the latter altogether.

Davidson supports his objection with two arguments. The first quickly dispatches the notion that a conceptual scheme in general could organize experience in general, by noting that it makes no sense for one object to organize another singular object. "We cannot attach a clear meaning to the notion of organizing a single object (the world, nature, etc.) unless that object is understood to contain or consist in other objects."[34] And of course, once we stipulate what those other objects are, there is little need to organize them conceptually (though one might reorganize them for certain purposes).

Davidson's second argument considers the more complicated notion that a conceptual scheme copes with, or fits, or faces experience. This notion entails a significantly different picture of what comprises a conceptual scheme, one that depends not on some point-by-point positioning or organizing of individual terms, but rather on the way sentences mutually articulate each other:

> When we turn from talk of organization to talk of fitting we turn our attention from the referential apparatus of language—predicates, quantifiers, variables, and singular terms—to whole sentences. It is sentences that predict (or are used to predict), sentences that cope or deal with things, that fit our sensory promptings, that can be compared or confronted with the evidence. It is sentences also that face the tribunal of experience, though of course they must face it together.[35]

Besides the picture of a conceptual scheme composed of a holistic field of sentences, Davidson also focuses on the theory of evidence that this conceptual scheme implies. "The general position is that sensory evidence provides all the *evidence* for the acceptance of sentences (where sentences may include whole theories)."[36] This position can easily be expanded into a general theory of what it means for a sentence or theory to be true, that is, into a theory of truth: "The point is that for a theory [or sentence] to fit or face up to the totality of possible sensory evidence is for that theory [or sentence] to be true."[37]

Needless to say, this scheme-content theory of truth is virtually a truism for most of us. Davidson's criticism of it is thus rather startling, and worth quoting at length.

> The trouble is that the notion of fitting the totality of experience, like the notion of fitting the facts, or of being true to the facts, adds nothing intelligible to the simple concept of being true. To speak

> of sensory experience rather than the evidence, or just the facts, expresses a view about the source or nature of evidence, but it does not add a new entity to the universe against which to test conceptual schemes. The totality of sensory evidence is what we want provided it is all the evidence there is; and all the evidence there is is just what it takes to make our sentences or theories true. Nothing, however, no *thing*, makes sentences and theories true: not experience, not surface irritations, not the world, can make a sentence true. *That* experience takes a certain course, that our skin is warmed or punctured, that the universe is finite, these facts, if we like to talk that way, make sentences and theories true. But this point is put better without mention of facts. The sentence "My skin is warm" is true if and only if my skin is warm. Here there is no reference to a fact, a world, an experience, or a piece of evidence.[38]

This passage can strike us as a mystifying blend of the radical and the trivial. To puzzle out just what Davidson is denying, and what he is proposing in its place, let us work through the passage from the bottom up.

"The sentence 'My skin is warm' is true if and only if my skin is warm." This tautology serves to introduce an alternative to the scheme-content, empiricist theory of truth: namely, the "disquotational" theory of truth. Davidson, following Alfred Tarski,[39] calls a sentence like the one above a T-sentence: it articulates a logical equation about what must be true in a "metalanguage" if a particular sentence in the "object language" (of that metalanguage) is true. We can generate such an equation by translating a quoted sentence in an object language into its corresponding sentence in that metalanguage; when the object language and the metalanguage are the same, we need only to take the sentence out of its quotation marks or to "disquote" it. Now proceeding from this formula, Davidson reasons that "the totality of such English [T-]sentences uniquely determines the extension of the concept of truth for English."[40] The trouble, of course, is that the totality of such T-sentences is infinite. In order to determine what it means for a sentence to be true in English, therefore, we would need a *finite* theory about how to generate an *infinite* set of T-sentences. Davidson, with Tarski, calls this constraint which any disquotational theory of truth must meet, Convention T.

> According to Tarski's Convention T, a satisfactory theory of truth
> for a language L must entail, for every sentence s of L, a theorem
> of the form "s is true if and only if p" where "s" is replaced by a
> description of s and "p" by s itself if L is English, and by a translation
> of s into English if L is not English.[41]

A theory of truth for L that meets the requirements of Convention
T would accordingly be able to generate and prove all T-sentence
theorems of sentences in L. Such a theory would also fix the meaning
of each word in a sentence to the extent that it can construct any
number of sentences in L that use a particular word without logical
contradiction. For this reason, Davidson considers this theory of
truth a theory of meaning as well, or a semantical theory of truth.

We need not investigate the ways that Davidson has proceeded
to develop such a theory in order to conclude that there appears to
be no reason *in principle* why such a theory cannot be formulated.
A corner has been turned; to the question of what it means for a
sentence or a theory to be true, of what makes sentences and theories
true, we can now answer: a disquotational theory of truth that accords
with Convention T will articulate, for each sentence or theory, a
T-sentence that explains what makes the sentence or theory true.

This answer has to be qualified, however. When we say that the
T-sentence explains what makes its object sentence true, that is not
quite accurate; the T-sentence rather stipulates what *other sentence*
in our language, the metalanguage of someone's object language,
we must logically hold to be true if we hold a quoted object *sentence*
to be true. With this in mind, Davidson's holistic approach to such
T-sentences becomes more understandable: it is only when we can
be confident in our ability to generate all possible T-sentences, to
translate another's language into our own, that we will be able to
know, metalinguistically, what else we may say is true if we say that
a particular sentence is true. But if this is indeed the way that
Davidson deals with the truth of sentences, then can we not continue
to ask: What *makes* the object sentence, which we initially hold to
be true, true? For surely we would be wrong to hold a sentence true
if it is in fact—that is, according to sensory evidence—false.

So it appears that, although we may use a disquotational theory of truth to generate T-sentences that render explicit the conditions for holding an object sentence to be true, we have to use an empiricist theory of truth to determine whether we should hold that object sentence to be true in the first place. In other words, we still need a theory of truth that not only matches sentences with other sentences, but also sentences with the world. Yet once Davidson has managed in this way to restrict, at least, the need for an empiricist theory of truth to that of determining the truth of the object sentence, he has effectively put that theory in mothballs. For he may now remind us of Quine's observation, cited earlier: "Any statement can be held true come what may, if we make drastic enough adjustments elsewhere in the system." It follows that "nothing makes sentences and theories true," that the truth of a particular sentence depends on whether we *decide* to hold it true and adjust our other sentences. Now what better way is there to calculate how drastic would be the adjustments required by holding a particular sentence true than, first, to lay out systematically a set of T-sentences appropriate to a specific situation, and second, to determine whether, if you experiment with holding certain of these T-sentences true and others false, any logical contradictions arise either in that set or in the metalanguage as a whole? It may not be possible in practice to hold true a set of relevant T-sentences that do not entail some contradictions somewhere, but obviously there is everything to be said for knowing what contradictions you have accepted and why.

Davidson uses the disquotational theory of truth, then, to develop Quine's concept of a "field of force" and Sellars's of the "logical space of reasons," and to purify them of their residual empiricism. Davidson accomplishes the latter task by criticizing the "third dogma" of empiricism, the dualism between empirical content and a conceptual scheme: he demonstrates that it is incoherent in one version (that is, as a theory about how individual terms are organized), and unnecessary in the other (that is, as a theory about what makes individual sentences true). He supplies us instead with a theory of truth whereby the truth of a particular sentence depends on our willingness to hold certain other sentences true, within a language that systematically subjects each sentence, and its component words, to truth and meaning conditions which can be articulated in a metalanguage of T-sentences. It is no longer necessary, therefore, to distinguish between a conceptual scheme and its empirical content, between theoretical and observational statements, between results and data, or finally, between subjective belief and objective evidence. When we deliberate about whether to hold a certain belief to be true, that is, to maintain it in the face of pressure to abandon it, we only have to deliberate about the costs and benefits of that belief to the logic of our language as a whole. Coherence with our other beliefs, and not correspondence with the world, becomes our main worry. Davidson thus enables us, and Rorty, finally to detach the problem of reason—that is: How should we justify our beliefs?—from the epistemological problem of consciousness—that is: How do our minds acquire beliefs that accurately represent the external world?—by reformulating the former problem as: How should we calculate the costs and benefits of the language formed by holding certain beliefs to be true?

(We should note that Davidson's rejection of empiricism, or of any empiricist theory of truth, does *not* entail a rejection of the idea that the utterance of a sentence is caused by identifiable events in the world. Like Quine, Davidson is comfortable with viewing the manner in which we use language as a form of behavior which ideally obeys physical laws. But again, these laws cannot account for how we judge or evaluate this manner, especially with respect to what one could have said. Thus a causal explanation of why you said a particular sentence, and a rational justification of the value of saying that sentence, form two, parallel accounts—framed in two language-games, as Wittgenstein might say—which cannot be reduced to one.)

Finally, the fourth step in Rorty's argument is to establish that we should calculate these costs and benefits not only with respect to how coherent a particular language of a belief may be, but more importantly, with respect to what such a more or less coherent language, moored alongside other languages available to us, may enable us to *do*. Rorty argues this by taking up the Wittgensteinian and Deweyan suggestion that we "treat alternative vocabularies as more like alternative tools than like bits of a jigsaw puzzle."[42] He glosses the import of this distinction as follows:

> To treat them [alternative vocabularies] as pieces of a puzzle is to assume that all vocabularies are dispensable, or reducible to other vocabularies, or capable of being united with all other vocabularies in one grand unified super vocabulary. If we avoid this assumption, we shall not be inclined to ask questions like "What is the place of consciousness in a world of molecules?" "Are colors more mind-dependent than weights?" . . . We should not try to answer such questions, for doing so leads either to the evident failures of reductionism or to the short-lived successes of expansionism. We should restrict ourselves to questions like "Does our use of these words get in the way of our use of those other words?" This is a question about whether our use of tools is inefficient, not a question about whether our beliefs are contradictory.[43]

When we move from a consideration of what beliefs we should hold in a language, to a consideration of which language we should speak, questions of coherence give way to pragmatic questions of utility. What the analogy of alternative vocabularies with alternative tools enables Rorty to do is to stress how our actions and our speech should support each other in practice; he would have failed to stress this had he used the analogy of alternative vocabularies with pieces of a puzzle. (Beliefs, though, *are* like such pieces.) He thus maintains the commonsensical view that a rational person is someone whose reasons for believing certain things, for saying certain things in a particular language, are consistent with her or his purposes in doing certain things, and vice versa.

Recognizing this obliges us, however, to expand the problem of reason from that of justifying sentences that express beliefs to that of justifying sentences that express in addition desires. We have to do this because, as Davidson also points out, a reason that purports to explain and justify some action, like that of using a language to utter some sentence, must weave together beliefs and desires.

> A reason rationalizes an action only if it leads us to see something the agent saw, or thought he saw, in his actions—some feature, consequence, or aspect of the action the agent wanted, desired, prized, held dear, thought dutiful, beneficial, obligatory, or agree-

able. We cannot explain why someone did what he did simply by saying the particular action appealed to him; we must indicate what it was about the action that appealed. Whenever someone does something for a reason, therefore, he can be characterized as (a) having some sort of pro attitude toward actions of a certain kind, and (b) believing (or knowing, perceiving, noticing, remembering) that his action is of that kind. [44]

Davidson goes on to note that:

> . . . under (a) are to be included desires, wantings, urges, promptings, and a great variety of moral views, aesthetic principles, economic prejudices, social conventions, and public and private goals and values in so far as these can be interpreted as attitudes of an agent directed toward actions of a certain kind. The word "attitude" does yeoman service here, for it must cover not only permanent character traits that show themselves in a lifetime of behavior, like love of children or a taste for loud company, but also the most passing fancy that prompts a unique action, like a sudden desire to touch a woman's elbow. [45]

It would seem that a large part of our "pro attitudes" consist of values to which our beliefs are helping us orient ourselves. Whereupon we need to ask ourselves: Where do these values come from?

One answer available to us is: from our will to power. This is where Rorty's reformulation of the problem of reason, then, brings us back to Nietzsche's critique of the idea of consciousness. In Rorty's hands, the problem has become: Does the language or vocabulary coherently formed by holding true certain beliefs help us to act to achieve certain valued ends? This way of putting it suggests that we could just as well bracket off the question of which beliefs to hold true, and deliberate more directly about what course of action to take to get what we want. The problem of reason may accordingly reduce to the question: Does performing such-and-such actions (including speaking actions) enable us to achieve certain valued ends? Significantly outside the scope of that question would be the status of the valued ends; we could not consider whether they are rational. Moreover, the last chapter's discussion suggests that we could further reduce this question to: Does performing such actions enable us to assert our will to power over the wills of other subjects?

This raises again the specter of perpetual, nihilistic antagonism that makes Nietzsche's conception of the will to power so threatening to our hopes for moderating social conflict rationally. Is Rorty's reformulation of the problem of reason, like Nietzsche's, a renunciation of reason? Is his pragmatism essentially tactical; is it, as the contemporary Nietzschean Michel Foucault has characterized instrumental reason in the human sciences, a continuation of war by other means?[46]

Rorty attempts to distance himself from this possibility. He shies away from talk of one will dominating another; he speaks instead of how differing wills may have to tolerate and compromise with each other in the interests of establishing a stable climate where they all may flourish. For him, the problem of justifying one's beliefs, in contrast to simply imposing and enforcing them, looms large as soon as it becomes prudent that one negotiate with others in terms acceptable to all. Justification then becomes entirely conversational. It no longer concerns what must be true, good, coherent, useful, and so on, but what others will let us take to be useful, and so on, what "our peers will, *ceteris paribus*, let us get away with saying."[47] Rorty tries to swerve off from the brink of Nietzschean nihilism, therefore, by making the problem of reason a thoroughly practical problem that arises in social contexts whose complexity resists prediction and control: we try to justify our beliefs when we are challenged by another, and those beliefs are justified when the other allows that they are. Only then, only after a satisfactory conversation that issues in mutually recognized, warranted beliefs, may we judge assuredly that a particular language has been effectively persuasive. At no point, though, would it be wise to consider a language warranted once and for all, since that language and its speakers always may have to answer to others in new situations. Justification is not an abstract, rule-governed guarantee, but an always-to-be-renewed, pragmatic achievement.

I shall assess the success of Rorty's move away from Nietzsche here in Chapter Five. In the meantime, we may consider how this philosophical idea of conversational reason transforms the task of cultural reform. "Criticism of one's culture can only be piecemeal and partial—never 'by reference to eternal standards'."[48] According to Rorty here, we criticize beliefs, desires, and actions in our culture in response to specific occasions; as those occasions alter or vanish our criticism may be revised or retracted. Such a conception of criticism precludes the skeptical possibility that we could doubt every single proposition that we might hold, all at once, once and for all. In the first place, to do that literally would take a proposition of near-infinite length. In the second place, we may no longer zero in on the fundamental axioms that govern the truth or falsity of every one of our beliefs, for Rorty denies that there are such axioms. No proposition is more essential to our belief system than any other. Consider an example of G.E. Moore: although we may be disposed on occasion to doubt, like Descartes and Kant, the proposition that there is an external world, these dispositions may be soon outweighed by more regular pressures to maintain the truth that "here is one hand," and to take that proposition to imply the existence of a world of external things.[49] It is next to impossible to predict which circumstances today would motivate one of us to abandon habitual beliefs in favor of radical alternatives, and which ones tomorrow would motivate one to reverse this movement; criticism does not move in an inherently progressive direction. This means, finally, that our beliefs bear not necessary but contingent conditions, and that the picture of criticism responsive to such conditions "threatens the neo-Kantian image of philosophy's relation to science and to culture."[50]

With these considerations in mind, then, Rorty abandons the idea that we need a philosophical tribunal to preside over our culture and its reform, and he reformulates the relation between philosophy and culture as a "hermeneutic" one. He distinguishes this relation from its neo-Kantian, epistemological counterpart as follows:

> Hermeneutics sees the relations between various discourses as those of strands in a possible conversation, a conversation which presupposes no disciplinary matrix which unites the speakers, but where the hope of agreement is never lost so long as the conversation lasts. This hope is not a hope for the discovery of antecedently existing

common ground, but *simply* the hope for agreement, or, at least, exciting and fruitful disagreement. Epistemology sees the hope of agreement as a token of the existence of common ground which, perhaps unbeknown to the speakers, unites them in a common rationality. For hermeneutics, to be rational is to be willing to refrain from epistemology—from thinking that there is a special set of terms in which all contributions to the conversation should be put—and to be willing to pick up the jargon of the interlocutor rather than translating it into one's own. For epistemology, to be rational is to find the proper set of terms into which all the contributions should be translated if agreement is to become possible. . . . Epistemology views the participants as united in what Oakeshott calls an *universitas*—a group united by mutual interests in achieving a common end. Hermeneutics views them as united in what he calls a *societas*—persons whose paths through life have fallen together, united by civility rather than by a common goal, much less by a common ground. [51]

I have quoted this lengthy passage because it details key contrasts between the neo-Kantian, epistemological philosopher and Rorty's post-Kantian, hermeneutic philosopher. (Rorty immediately goes on to acknowledge that his use of the term "hermeneutic" departs in significant respects from the way the term has been used from Schleiermacher through Dilthey to Gadamer; for our purposes, however, little hangs on this difference.) Where the epistemological philosopher searches for universal truths, her or his hermeneutic counterpart learns multiple languages for describing things. Where the former looks for the right side in a clash of opinions, the latter hopes to negotiate an acceptable and useful compromise. Where the former seeks to discover the common foundation of our cultural enterprises, the latter attempts to build (temporary) bridges for cooperation, or at least tolerance, between those enterprises. And finally, despite these differences, the latter is no less "rational" than the former. Indeed, regarding the conversational core of hermeneutics, Rorty remarks:

. . . I want to give a very high-toned sense to "conversation." . . . If you think of the conversation of mankind not as a chat; but as standing for the whole human enterprise—culture, if you like—

then "conversation" is a perfectly reasonable word for what we do to be saved.[52]

In particular, conversation is what we do to build up what Sellars calls "we-intentions."[53] These are intentions that have the following form: we intend that if one of us is in circumstances C, then that person will do A. Sellars argues that we express such intentions whenever we make moral judgments; as his argument is highly technical, and presupposes familiarity with a specialized literature, I shall only mention three of its main claims which bear on our discussion. One is that we-intentions render perspicuous our sense that moral judgments challenge us to act on principle; they have the force of a categorical imperative. This is because what is being intended is that one *do* A *whenever* one is in circumstances C—not that one consider doing A, and not that one do A if one is in C and in the mood. A second pertinent claim is that we-intentions capture our sense that moral judgments are intersubjective and controversial. This follows from the fact that it is *we* who are supposedly intending a course of action; so if I say (in so many words), "we intend that if one of us is in circumstances C, then that person will do A," and you say, "we intend that if . . . C, then that person will not do A," then one of us must be wrong, inasmuch as we are both talking about what "we" intend. These two claims, then, preserve the traditional force of our moral judgments from emotivism (the idea that such judgments are at bottom merely subjective expressions of feelings or behavioral dispositions) and relativism (the idea that differing judgments stem from the incommensurable circumstances of the judges such that there is no neutral, common framework for resolution). A third claim of Sellars, finally, is that moral judgments are a species of practical judgment that *logically cause* action. For example, the following sequence of sentences logically concludes in an expression of intention that normally should cause the speaker or thinker of the sentences to actually do A.

(1.) "I am (or will be) in C."
(2.) "We intend that if one of us is in C, then that person will do A."

(3.) "Therefore we intend that I do A."
(4.) "Therefore I intend to do A."

This chain of reasoning, however schematic, exhibits how a we-intention may help explain and justify an action, and so play the role of a Davidsonian pro attitude and of a Nietzschean value. Unlike the cases we looked at from Davidson and Nietzsche, however, the reason for acting here is explicitly tied to an expression of what *we* want or intend or value, not just what I value. Sellars's argument for we-intentions, then, permits us not only to defend most of our traditional claims about moral judgments, but also to absorb Nietzsche's insight that those judgments, and our values in general, are based on desires that we actively affirm, *without impugning the intersubjective dimension of those judgments and values.* There is no reason why my values, based on the desires I affirm, cannot harmonize with your values, based on the we-intentions affirmed by you as well as me.

Of course nothing that I have said implies that Sellars's claims for we-intentions are problem-free. Nothing, especially, gives them the status of guarantees, for we-intentions, like the rest of our provisional beliefs and desires, may be overturned. Rorty does not flinch from this possibility, and, with Sartre, takes a hard look at what may lie in store for us:

> Tomorrow, after my death, certain people may decide to establish fascism, and the others may be cowardly or miserable enough to let them get away with it. At that moment, fascism will be the truth of man, and so much the worse for us. In reality, things will be as much as man has decided they are.[54]

The only thing that will save us from, or damn us to, this fate is ourselves. And it is precisely the merit of we-intentions, Rorty notes, to make this bottom line unmistakable.[55] Rorty champions Sellars's formulation for trailblazing a way to display how the health of our cultural values depends on how well each of us appreciates our "we-ness," our ethical solidarity. The formulation provides us with a conception of our values that accords with the conversational conception of reason. It thus extends to us a fighting chance, at least, to defend our values from nihilistic reasoning, and it promises to fortify them with what each of us, thrown together, hope for our society in the teeth of possible catastrophes around the corner.

The argument of this chapter, then, broaches a way out of the Kantian conception of a philosophical education for cultural reform. It suggests that we may transform the problem of reason so as to free that problem from the problem of consciousness, leaving the notions of mind, of a theory of knowledge, and of philosophy as a tribunal of pure reason without a job to do. In the changed relations between philosophy and culture, our values need no longer be grounded on an epistemological foundation of knowledge. We are free to make them instead the products, and the stakes, of an educational effort to build a culture of conversation, especially one that would promote ethical solidarity.

Nevertheless, there is still the Nietzschean connection to worry about. We may remain disturbed that Rorty's philosophy apparently allows room for a Nietzschean subject who could simply not care about justifying her or his beliefs and actions to others, and who could exclusively concern herself or himself with self-centered desires or values. If that is the case, then what could motivate such people to overrule their "I-intentions" with we-intentions? What could motivate any one of us to do that?

Before tackling these and related questions, it would help if we could get a clearer sense of what the individual subject looks like in Rorty's world, and especially of how closely, if at all, it resembles the Nietzschean subject. To this end, I propose that we first complete our criticism of the Cartesian legacy, and firm up our new point of departure, by working out what the transformation of the problem of reason means to the traditionally associated problem of personhood. Should we leave this latter problem attached to the problem of consciousness, leaving both to wither away? Or should we transform it correspondingly, in order to reattach it to our new problem of reason? These questions will form the themes of our next chapter.

4

FROM CONSCIOUSNESS TO EDIFICATION

By the close of the first part of *Philosophy and the Mirror of Nature*, Rorty had already announced his intention to reformulate the problem of personhood in non-Cartesian, and by extension non-Kantian, terms. Yet before we follow him in this enterprise, we need to assure ourselves that it is still necessary. Why consider the problem of personhood anything other than a species of that of reason? Is the former problem any different in kind from other problems of justifying your beliefs—in this case, your beliefs about the nature of personhood—in the course of conversing with others?

It is not, and the ensuing discussion should, as a matter of course, be subjected to various conversations testing reasons. Yet Rorty singles out the problem of personhood for special attention because his reformulation of the problem of reason cannot by itself make the case that we need a new conception of philosophical education for cultural reform. For that to be made, he needs to bolster that reformulation with an account of what we must be like for it to fit us. Otherwise, we might continue to assume certain things about our personhood which clash with the idea that our reason and philosophical learning are basically conversational.

> It is difficult to imagine that any activity would be entitled to bear the name "philosophy" if it had nothing to do with knowledge—if it were not in some sense a theory of knowledge, or a method for getting knowledge, or at least a hint as to where some supremely important kind of knowledge might be found. The difficulty stems

from a notion shared by Platonists, Kantians, and positivists: that man has an essence—namely to discover essences. The notion that our chief task is to mirror accurately, in our own Glassy Essence, the universe around us is the complement of the notion, common to Democritus and Descartes, that the universe is made up of very simple, clearly and distinctly knowable things, knowledge of whose essences provides the master vocabulary which provides commensuration of all discourses.[1]

Rorty recognizes that what makes the epistemological conception of philosophical education so appealing lies not merely in that conception's claims to internal coherence—claims on which our last two chapters cast doubt—but especially in its capacity to meet the educational needs of a certain conception of our personhood, one according to which we are beings whose essence is "to mirror accurately the universe around us," to possess reflective *consciousness*. He is troubled by the idea that, as long as we take this conception of personhood for granted, we will always find it supremely useful to converse first and foremost in epistemological terms, to strive to make culture a more accurate mirror of nature. Thus his argument that reasons function in their languages as so many conversational, rhetorical tools, rather than as pieces of a puzzle, might nevertheless allow a particular language of knowledge, a particular language geared to assemble pieces of a puzling mirror image of the world, to dominate over our other linguistic tools, and even to claim to constitute the ground of our culture and the principles of a philosophical tribunal which would preside over that culture. To block this possibility, therefore, he concludes that "this classic picture of human beings as mirrorers must be set aside before epistemologically centered philosophy can be set aside."[2] He attempts to make his reformulation of the problem of reason stick by reformulating, in turn, the problem of personhood set up by the Cartesian notion of our essential consciousness.

Rorty comes at this latter problem from the angle of what it means to be a self. The problem of personhood, he argues, boils down to the problem of how we each develop a sense of selfhood, a problem which swings free of any account of our consciousness. As with his reformulation of the problem of reason, he maps out a position with respect to ideas which he borrows from other thinkers. Once again, then, we will fill out his pattern of allusion and interpretation, and, in line with his new conception of reason, we will examine the resultant, reconstructed argument less for how literally faithful it is to the texts it considers, and more for how shrewdly it employs those texts to construct a coherent and useful conception of the self. I should caution at the outset that the argument here is less tidy than the one we examined in the last chapter, having a more groping, speculative cast. Yet I hope that, as we are borne along by its imaginative leaps, we will start to realize how aptly this kind of exploratory writing suits the self-conceiving purposes of the writer.

Rorty opens his case by making "hermeneutics" the common locus of attempts to reformulate the problem of reason and the problem of personhood. He remarks that the philosopher primarily responsible for forging the link between hermeneutics and our personhood was Hans-Georg Gadamer:

> Gadamer is asking, roughly, what conclusions might be drawn from the fact that we have to practice hermeneutics—from the "hermeneutic phenomenon" as a fact about people which the epistemological tradition has tried to shunt aside. . . . His book [*Truth and Method*] is a redescription of man which tries to place the classic picture within a larger one, and thus to "distance" the standard philosophical [i.e., epistemological] problematic rather than offer a set of solutions to it.[3]

Recall that by the "hermeneutic phenomenon," Rorty means the phenomenon of conversational, as opposed to epistemological, reason. He is asserting here not only that hermeneutics is an everyday practice, but that we may actually consider epistemological inquiry a branch of hermeneutics. To follow up on these claims, then, he needs to determine how we may leave behind the notion of our mirroring, "Glassy Essence," which privileges epistemological reason, to pursue a notion of personhood that would privilege hermeneutic, conversational reason.

One might expect Rorty at this point to advance an account of our "Conversational Essence." (Indeed, this is arguably the tack that Gadamer himself takes in his discussion of "the conversational

81

structure of hermeneutic understanding.")⁴ Yet he declines this gambit, presumably because its own claims about our "essence" would have obstructed his holistic view of all the propositional claims that could be made about us. So instead, Rorty looks around for a conception of personhood that would not require essentialist claims at all.

He finds what he needs in Gadamer's "romantic notion of man as self-creative."⁵ This notion steers us away from the notion that consciousness is one of our essential properties, and toward the exercise of conversational reason. How? By inviting us to reconceive of thinking:

> . . . [Gadamer substitutes] the notion of *Bildung* (education, self-formation) for that of "knowledge" as the goal of thinking.⁶

In this key statement, Rorty underlines how Gadamer's notion of self-creativity entails a reformulation of *what is at stake* for thinking. Where before it was epistemological knowledge, which suited our nature as conscious beings, now it is *education* conceived as "self-formation," which suits the needs of a being that lacks any essential nature. Rorty develops this conception as follows:

> To say that we become different people, that we "remake" ourselves as we read more, talk more, and write more, is simply a dramatic way of saying that the sentences which become true of us by virtue of such activities are often more important to us than the sentences which become true of us when we drink more, earn more, and so on. The events which make us able to say new and interesting things about ourselves are, in this nonmetaphysical sense, more "essential" to us (at least to us relatively leisured intellectuals, inhabiting a stable and prosperous part of the world) than the events which change our shapes or our standards of living. . . . Gadamer develops his notion of *wirkungsgeschichtliches Bewusstein* (the sort of consciousness of the past which changes us) to characterize an attitude interested not so much in what is out there in the world, or in what happened in history, as in what we can get out of nature and history for our own uses. In this attitude, getting the facts right (about atoms and the void, or about the history of Europe) is merely propaedeutic to finding a new and more interesting way of expressing ourselves, and thus of coping with the world. From the educational, as opposed

to the epistemological or the technological, point of view, the way things are said is more important than the possession of truths.

Since "education" sounds a bit too flat, and *Bildung* a bit too foreign, I shall use "edification" to stand for this project of finding new, better, more interesting, more fruitful ways of speaking.[7]

This is a puzzling, at times startling, passage, one whose principal ideas demand elucidation before we can feel comfortable doing anything with them. One thing, though, is clear at the outset: Rorty's new conception of personhood connects linguistic activities of "reading more, talking more, and writing more," of "saying new and interesting things about ourselves," of "expressing ourselves," and so forth, with more overarching activities of "self-formation" and "remaking" oneself. To elucidate this passage, and the conception of edification in particular, let us try to get the connection between these two sorts of activities more in focus. It will be helpful to consider the following questions.

First: How can Rorty substitute edification for knowledge as the goal of thinking? Would not the acquisition of knowledge by thinking be a necessary element, if not the sum and substance, of edification? And conversely, would not any acquisition of knowledge entail some measure of edification? In short, how can he conceive of edification and knowledge as being intrinsically separate from one another, and thus capable of being substituted for one another for whatever reason?

Second: How can Rorty join edification or self-formation to various activities that remake us? Would not the goal of self-formation be to create a self that has no prior form, to form a self out of what is not yet a self? But does not the idea of "being remade," or "remaking oneself," on the contrary, imply that the self in question already exists in a form which has merely to be rebuilt? Do not activities that remake us, then, presuppose edification as an accomplished fact?

And third: Why should Rorty claim that "remaking ourselves as we read more, talk more, and write more" is "more important to us" than activities that remake "our shapes or our standards of living"? Would it not be more plausible to claim that these linguistic activities are in fact less important than activities that permit us to become "relatively leisured" and to "inhabit a stable and prosperous part of the world?" For Rorty himself seems to admit that such a station in life is a necessary condition for appreciating the importance of such linguistic activities, let alone for engaging in them in any sustained fashion.

We can make a start on the first set of questions by noting that Rorty does acknowledge that the acquisition of knowledge is an important first step toward edification.

> The hermeneutic point of view, from which the acquisition of truth dwindles in importance, and is seen as a component of education, is possible only if we once stood at another point of view. Education has to start from acculturation. So the search for objectivity and the self-conscious awareness of the social practices in which objectivity consists are necessary first steps in becoming *gebildet* [edified]. . . . Later perhaps, we may put less value on "being in touch with reality" but we can afford that only after having passed through stages of implicit, and then explicit and self-conscious, conformity to the norms of the discourses going on around us.[8]

Rorty supposes this a "banal point," but it may be informative to amplify a bit *why* education has to start with acculturation and conformity. In this regard, we may turn to the way Gadamer reinterprets the significance of a thinker's prejudices and preconceptions for the purposes of *Bildung*. According to Gadamer, and following the example of Enlightenment philosophers, we normally consider such prejudices to be opinionative obstacles to grasping an object of study clearly and distinctly; by all rights, then, they ought to be eliminated. Hermeneutic thinkers, however, gradually came to appreciate how prejudices and preconceptions were attached to those implicit interests (pro attitudes), rooted in our history, that motivate our interpretive acts, interests without which we could not comprehend the importance of anything. These interests become recognizable when we, on the one hand, scrupulously acknowledge the historical distance between the object and ourselves, thus exposing the preconceptions that would gloss over that distance, and when we, on the other hand, track the causes of these preconceptions to the same historical events that produced the object, thus binding ourselves to the object in a common tradition. Hermeneutic thinkers labor in this way to keep us in a dialogue with objects that reveals our historical identity, and viable possibilities for continuing our traditions. Gadamer calls this dialogue "effective history" (*Wirkungsgeschichte*): it is the history of how events in the world situated us, a world whose features bear the traces of the inherited interests, in our prejudices, that direct the way we interpret and talk about what we find in our world.[9] History is thus not a dead, positive object of study—what has been in the removed past, once and for all—but an ongoing, dialectical event of *Bildung*, self-formation, via acculturation. This is why education begins, like it or not, in conformity with what others have thought about, and been interested in, before us.

Of course we hope that education will not end there. As we become more conscious of our effective history, as we grow in "effective historical consciousness" (*wirkungsgeschichtliches Bewusstein*), possibilities for changing as well as continuing that history open up for us. Now we do not have to act on those additional possibilities; we may content ourselves with self-consciously reproducing our traditions. Yet we may choose to react against parts of those traditions, after, and even because, we have recognized them as *the* traditions that formed us. Our effective historical consciousness, our education based on acculturation—to return to Rorty's more familiar idiom—may lead us either to preserve and extend our traditions, or to criticize and transform them. Rorty elaborates this alternative as follows:

> I want now to generalize this contrast between philosophers whose work is essentially constructive and those whose work is essentially reactive. I shall thereby develop a contrast between philosophy which centers in epistemology and the sort of philosophy which takes its point of departure from suspicion about the pretensions of epistemology. This is the contrast between "systematic" and "edifying" philosophies.[10]

To sharpen this contrast, let us first articulate the elements on the epistemological, systematic side. Rorty hooks these together as follows:

> In every sufficiently reflective culture, there are those who single out one area, one set of practices, and see it as the paradigm human activity. They then try to show how the rest of culture can profit from this example. In the mainstream of the Western philosophical tradition, this paradigm has been *knowing*—possessing justified true beliefs, or, better yet, beliefs so intrinsically persuasive as to make justification unnecessary. . . . A "mainstream" Western philosopher typically says: Now that such-and-such a line of inquiry has had such a stunning success, let us reshape all inquiry, and all of culture, on its model, thereby permitting objectivity and rationality to prevail in areas previously obscured by convention, superstition, and the lack of a proper epistemological understanding of man's ability accurately to represent nature.[11]

In this sense, the "mainstream" philosopher is constructive insofar as he builds up a line of inquiry that promises to "reshape all inquiry, and all of culture, on its model." His warrant for undertaking such a project is epistemological: he wants "objectivity and rationality to prevail," thus reinforcing the claim that knowing constitutes the paradigm human activity and that consciousness constitutes our essential personhood. His success may be gauged by how much of his culture he can cover with his model language without serious contradiction, that is, how systematically extensive he can make his philosophy. Hopefully, as a result of his efforts, the "mainstream of the Western philosophical tradition" will perpetuate itself, and its interest in epistemology stay vital.

Rorty juxtaposes to these philosophers those who are "edifying":

> On the periphery of the history of modern philosophy, one finds figures who, without forming a "tradition," resemble each other in their distrust of the notion that man's essence is to be a knower of essences. . . . They are often dubious about progress, and especially about the latest claim that such-and-such a discipline has at last made the nature of human knowledge so clear that reason will now spread throughout the rest of human activity. These writers have kept alive the suggestion that even when we have justified true belief about everything we want to know, we may have no more than conformity to the norms of the day. They have kept alive the historicist sense that this century's "superstition" was the last century's triumph of reason, as well as the relativist sense that the latest vocabulary, borrowed from the latest scientific achievements, may not express privileged representations of essences, but be just another

of the potential infinity of vocabularies in which the world can be described.[12]

Edifying philosophers, unlike their systematic counterparts, acknowledge that epistemological philosophy is not the paradigm human activity, but, at any moment in any of its particular incarnations, "just another of the potential infinity of vocabularies in which the world can be described." For this reason, they consider the project of constructing and systematically stretching a model inquiry to blanket all of culture, when detached from its (built-up) epistemological warrant, to be a project that simply "conforms to the norms of the day." If and when conformity to those norms no longer proves useful, they are thus ready to try to depart from the mainstream of Western philosophy in diverse ways.

> Great systematic philosophers are constructive and offer arguments. Great edifying philosophers are reactive and offer satires, parodies, aphorisms. They know their work loses its point when the period they are reacting against is over. They are *intentionally* peripheral. Great systematic philosophers, like great scientists, build for eternity. Great edifying philosophers destroy for the sake of their own generation. Systematic philosophers want to put their subject on the secure path of a science. Edifying philosophers want to keep space open for the sense of wonder which poets can sometimes cause—wonder that there is something new under the sun, something which is *not* an accurate representation of what was already there, something which (at least for the moment) cannot be explained and can barely be described.[13]

In contrast to an education oriented to preserve or advance our traditions, then, we may propose an education that reacts against some of them. Such an education would check the impulse to apologize for epistemologically based paradigms across the board, and would strive to hatch something new by cracking the crust of systematic conventions. These conventions threaten to inhibit our appreciation of and sensitivity to the various strange, often unadmitted, but potentially useful possibilities open to us for acting in our culture.

Because Rorty distinguishes, for the purposes of thinking about what our acculturation makes possible for us, a more pluralistic and pathbreaking education from a more uniformly conservative or progressive one—we can talk here of "conservative" and "progressive" in the same breath to the degree that both tendencies claim to be responding to the tides of historical continuity—he is able to distinguish edification from knowledge as the goal of thinking. He proceeds from the historical observation that the epistemological tradition, it so happens, plays a leading role in the effective history that initially situates us Westerners in our world, in the acculturation that initially causes us to identify ourselves as "Westerners." This means that we can use our education in our tradition to further that tradition's epistemological aspirations, understood faithfully. Yet even as we inherit and loyally take up those ongoing projects, we must also accept responsibility for other possibilities of dropping or drastically altering them. The kind of education that would encourage us to take responsibility for such heterogeneous, ambiguous possibilities in our history, rather than stipulate that we remain believers in fixed ends, would be one that encourages us to edify ourselves. As we thus take charge of our own education, in contrast to being passively acculturated, we realize that the acquisition of knowledge is only one of several promising avenues for contributing to cultural reform. *Knowledge need not be the principal coin of our culture.* Thus the edification of each one of us depends on considering as wide a spectrum of these differing possibilities as one can; for this reason, therefore, edification amounts in a sense to a "larger" goal for thinking than that of knowledge. It should be added, however, that the language of edification and that of knowledge are more precisely incommensurable; they do different things and share no (nonvacuous) common ground.

We will perhaps always need to be reassured, however, that the "destructive" devices set loose by edifying philosophers leave something in their wake besides fragmented rubble. Hence the call for modernist "Whiggish" historians, hermeneutic counterparts to epistemologists, who can restore continuity to the tradition by revising its account to show how past events paved the way for a revolution in progress. Such historians argue that events and features once considered incidental may not only hold the key to innovation in the present, but also to a reinterpretation and reappreciation of the past. They help us perceive both how our understanding of the tradition is revolutionized, and how revolutions are made by tradition. But what they are pointing out are interpretive possibilities in history, not fixed truths. A good example of such a history would be Rorty's own account of Enlightenment philosophy, an account which reinterprets, problematizes, and revolutionizes that tradition by focusing not on the victory of secular, scientific reason, but on the defeated attempts to solve the problem of consciousness. To identify ourselves as children of that philosophical project, then, is to accept responsibility for coping with a problem that unsettles and challenges its current pieties.

Both Whiggish historians and edifying thinkers acknowledge that we lack any essential personhood—a lack that the notion of consciousness was supposed to fill, but could not—and they affirm projects to fashion multiple, temporary notions of personhood. Indeed, once we stress the multiple and temporary character of such notions, it is difficult to avoid stressing the notion that such notions will belong to various selves. When personhood becomes something that develops contingently, selfhood becomes central. But to understand Rorty's idea of self, we need to confront our second set of questions concerning the connection between linguistic activities and edifying ones. How is the project to create or form oneself related to activities that purportedly remake us in language?

Rorty discusses this connection at length in the second chapter of his book *Contingency, Irony, and Solidarity*, entitled "The Contingency of Selfhood." There he works out an idea of how selfhood develops out of a project of redescription that confronts and responds to our mortality. The chapter opens with some stanzas from Philip Larkin, in which the narrator muses about the tragically unsatisfying process of self-understanding: how it develops self-control out of the things that impressed themselves on your behavior and shaped you, but how it is powerless to overcome your final separateness and mortality.[14]

Rorty takes these stanzas to express the poet's fear of dying. Rorty specifies that this is the fear that the poet's unique "lading-list," which "made his I different from all other I's," will be lost to the world; that what gave meaning to his life will be destroyed.[15] Proceeding from this premise, he then considers two ways of coping with the fear.

The first is to discover those elements of ourselves that transcend our differences from others, elements that "would be necessary, essential, telic, constitutive of what it is to be a human"; in other words, to solve the old problem of personhood.[16] If we can recognize that underlying our apparent dissimilarities there is a true, common essence that joins all people at all times, then we will be able to console ourselves with the idea that the part of us that must die— each one's individuality—is a relatively inessential, accidental, animalistic aspect of who we are, and hence not that important, not to be treasured or missed. A classic example of such an argument would be that in Plato's *Phaedo*, where the metaphysical inquiry into ideals is equated with an education in learning how to die. On this view, we need not fear that our essence could die; we could reassure ourselves that ultimately we are immortal. And as we discussed in Chapter Two, Descartes identified this essence with our conscious mind.

Rorty interprets the poet to be yearning to grasp such an essence, especially since the poet repudiates any satisfaction or gain in tracing the idiosyncratic features impressed upon his life. But can such an essence, such a vision of the true world, be attained? Particularly given the antinomies surrounding the problem of consciousness? And, assuming that we have not yet attained it, what gives us the idea that there *is* some true world that we could attain a vision of? What if there were *only* the misleading world?

At this point, Rorty once more aligns himself with Nietzsche. He reminds us that it was Nietzsche, above all, who brought these doubts to the attention of modern thinkers. Consider, for example, the chapter in Nietzsche's *Twilight of the Idols* entitled "How the 'True World' Finally Became a Fable."[17] After running through the first two stages, Platonic and Christian, of this metamorphosis, Nietzsche summarizes the step from the third, Kantian, "Königsbergian" stage, where the thing-in-itself is postulated to save the epistemological project, to a fourth stage, where the thing-in-itself, and the true world that depends on it, lose their hold on us.

> (3.) The true world—unattainable, indemonstrable, unpromisable, but the very thought of it—a consolation, an obligation, an imperative.
> (At bottom, the old sun, but seen through mist and skepticism. The idea has become elusive, pale, Nordic, Königsbergian.)
> (4.) The true world—unattainable? At any rate, unattained. And being unattained, also *unknown*. Consequently, not consoling, redeeming, or obligating: how could something unknown obligate us?[18]

Skipping a step, we come to a characteristically Nietzschean conclusion.

> (6.) The "true" world—an idea which is no longer good for anything, not even obligating—an idea which has become useless and superfluous—*consequently*, a refuted idea: let us abolish it![19]

But if we abandon the epistemological quest for that world, for the realm of the immortal soul or consciousness underlying the appearance of our material bodies, then what understanding of ourselves would be left? Is there any other sense of personhood that could help us cope with the fear of death?

It turns out that Nietzsche also provides us with a second way of dealing with this fear and of understanding ourselves, one which Rorty endorses.

> He [Nietzsche] hoped that, once we realized that Plato's "true world" was just a fable, we would seek consolation, at the moment of death, not in having transcended the animal condition but in being that peculiar sort of dying animal who, by describing himself in his own terms, had created himself. More exactly, he would have created the only part of himself that mattered by constructing his own mind.[20]

Instead of seeking to transcend his individual, mortal animality, Nietzsche affirms it. He claims that a significant part of it, his mind, was his own creative achievement. In a limited but crucial sense, then, Nietzsche can cope with his fear of death by taking satisfaction in what he has made of his contingent existence. Unlike Larkin's,

Nietzsche's lading-list is not to be despised for its impermanence, but to be celebrated, as he dies, for its irreducible differences from any other list, for its irreplicable accomplishments.

But this take on Nietzsche spins off more riddles. What does Rorty (and presumably Nietzsche) mean when he claims that "by describing himself in his own terms, [Nietzschean man] had created himself"? And how do these activities of describing and creating amount to "constructing his own mind"? Rorty starts to clarify these strange assertions by explaining the crucial role played in the process of self-creation by metaphoric invention.

> The process of coming to know oneself, confronting one's contingency, tracking one's causes home, is identical with the process of inventing a new language—that is, of thinking up some new metaphors. For any *literal* description of one's individuality, which is to say any use of an inherited language-game for this purpose, will necessarily fail. One will not have traced that idiosyncrasy home but will merely have managed to see it as not idiosyncratic after all, as a specimen reiterating a type, a copy or replica of something which has already been identified. To fail as a poet—and thus, for Nietzsche, to fail as a human being—is to accept somebody else's description of oneself, to execute a previously prepared program, to write, at most, elegant variations on previously written poems. So the only way to trace home the causes of one's being as one is would be to tell a story about one's causes in a new language. [21]

This passage clears up some of the confusion surrounding the identification of "self-formation" with "remaking oneself as we read more, talk more, and write more." As we, proceeding from the language passed down from society (including the family, the school, the neighborhood, and so on), take various stabs at a "better" future, and are affected in turn by such acts, we acquire a growing self-awareness and sense of where we are—we learn to master that language and identify ourselves in it. We start to understand the things and events that shaped us. This understanding enables each one of us to distinguish, from the customary codes of our society, the accidental idiosyncrasies which have stuck in our speech, and to liken such idiosyncrasies to those in our other behavior. Now if you find these idiosyncrasies likable, and more significant to you than the standard forms of speaking and behaving you have inherited, you may wish to modify some of these forms with tics and flourishes that you have cultivated in an "original" fashion. You might thus attempt to redescribe yourself—to describe yourself in terms different from those by which we conventionally or "literally" describe people like you—so as to stamp your life with such marks of distinction. In this way, then, each one of us can create a unique sense of selfhood, one's own self, by redescribing the self our society identifies in us—the self we have learned to talk about in literal terms—in one's own invented terms. As paradoxical as it sounds, we *create* our *own* selves by *redescribing* our *given* selves.

Such experiments in redescription stand a chance, moreover, of creating mutant forms of language which could help others to evolve their own special features. Although which particular bits of language will have this effect on us is virtually impossible to predict, metaphorical sentences are generally useful, for they get listeners to look at sides of things we normally neglect, without exactly telling them what they will find. Rorty, with Davidson, understands metaphor to be an odd use of words that carry standard meanings rather than some special "metaphorical" meanings. [22] This view entails that most metaphorical sentences are simply false (for instance, "He was a real pig."), hence the shock they are apt to communicate to us. Yet— in a deft twist on the positivist theory of meaning—Davidson and Rorty hold that the patent falsity of such sentences serves to signal listeners that a different, nonpropositional language-game is being played with another goal in mind (to use a Wittgensteinian figure). Although it is impossible for a sentence formulated in an old language to constitute a *reason in that language* to move to a different language, metaphorical sentences may act on us "irrationally," and cause us to transcend a particular language as we grope for ways to respond to them. They are vulnerable, therefore, to being condemned for reasons that beg the question in favor of the language from which they are trying to move away. But their actual value is in their provocations, which are the instruments by which we may experiment on ourselves to remake ourselves. They suit Emerson's insight into education: "Truly speaking, it is not instruction, but provocation, that I can receive from another soul."[23] As provocative idiosyncrasies, they point to exits from the standard language, and distinguish their users from conventional speakers.

To recap: each time we express our unique, changing lives in fitting, metaphorical language, we remake our given selves, form our own selves, and innovate the ways any self can express itself. Rorty rhymes, so to speak, the self who takes advantage of such opportunities with Harold Bloom's conception of the "strong poet" who wins poetic originality.[24] According to Bloom, every poet was a reader before a writer, one who learned to appreciate poetry through the compelling work of one or more (but not indiscriminately many) precursors. Such precursors impress the initiate with what it is possible to accomplish. As soon as the reader of poetry is filled with the desire to write herself comparably accomplished poetry, however, her attitude to the precursors becomes charged with ambivalence. On the one hand, her love of (a certain kind of) poetry remains bound to a formative love of the precursors' poems; this love continues to shape her sense of what in her efforts could compel. On the other hand, her sense of her own originality, her conviction that her poetry is not superfluous and can make a difference to some audience, depends on her ability to keep her precursors from completely anticipating her, alienating her from her own inspiration, and rendering her work a belated copy of what has already been done better. Bloom calls this ambivalence the poet's "anxiety of influence." He tries to show how strong poets, such as Milton, Shelley, Hardy, and others defeat such anxiety by contriving unconsciously, as in a dreamwork, to trope the sentences, perceptions, sentiments, and ideas of their precursors in new but equally compelling ways, much as one might symbolically gratify a repressed desire in an ingenious fashion. Against the myth of the genius who creates *ex nihilo*, he counterposes the conception of the "revisionary agonist," one who struggles with her precursors to wrest innovative, "strong misreadings" of their work that she could claim as her own.[25] Such a figure provides Rorty with a powerful metaphor for how any self redescribes herself or himself in her or his own terms.

(I have deliberately used the feminine pronoun above in order to raise the question, at least, of whether Bloom's account of how you forge your poetic voice can be plausibly extended to the tradition of women's literature, and so whether this conception of self-formation is not too patriarchal. On the one hand, Sandra M. Gilbert and Susan Gubar, in their groundbreaking study, *The Madwoman in the Attic,* have argued that Bloom's theory precisely illuminates an important difference between the influence anxieties of men and women writers. Female initiates have to take on precursors who are almost exclusively male, and so have to cope additionally with the self-consciousness of being an incongruous interloper, of being perhaps unsuited by gender to a literary vocation.[26] On the other hand, Rorty has argued that this conception of revisionary agonistics, of self-formation, can actually help us to appreciate the ongoing project to form a new voice in feminist criticism in general, and in the work of Catharine MacKinnon in particular.)[27]

This argument, incidentally, casts further light on how Rorty reads and appropriates for his purposes the work of Descartes, Davidson, Gadamer, and others. It shows why it would be beside the point to accuse Rorty, without further ado, of misreading these authors. Indeed, the argument extends to him the liberty to (willfully) identify Harold Bloom's strong poet with the self in general, and with himself, and other wondering philosophers, in particular:

> The wonder in which Aristotle believed philosophy to begin was wonder at finding oneself in a world larger, stronger, nobler than oneself. The fear in which Bloom's poets begin is the fear that one might end one's days in such a world, a world one never made, an inherited world. The hope of such a poet is that what the past tried to do to her she will succeed in doing to the past: to make the past itself, including those very causal processes which blindly impressed all her own behavings, bear *her* impress. Success in that enterprise . . . is what Bloom calls "giving birth to oneself."[28]

In the next two chapters, we will ponder at more length the contrast that Rorty opens up here between Aristotelian, or more generally metaphysical, wonder, and his and Harold Bloom's fear; we will consider in particular what this contrast implies about the desire to which a liberal education should respond. For the meantime, we may proceed to the question broached earlier, of what these linguistic activities of self-formation have to do with constructing one's own mind. Is the mind made up of words rather than consciousness? As we saw in the last chapter, Sellars's psychologist Jones suggests that the distinction between mind and body amounts not to a difference in substance, but to one in how their descriptive terms are used methodologically. Rorty pursues this lead, and further distances himself from the Cartesian notion of personhood, by adopting Davidson's account of how mind and body are related, one called "anomalous monism."[29]

Davidson remarks that we may describe acts of the mind such as thinking, believing, wanting, and so on, in two fashions. First, we may talk about them as mental events (of, for example, "thinking," "believing," and so forth). Or second, we may talk about them as physical events (of, for example, "a specific neurochemical reaction in the brain caused by the irritation of a specific nerve ending"). Either type of description is translatable into the language of the other, but definitive features of these different descriptive languages put certain conditions on such translations.

The first is ontological: all mental events are physical events, but not all physical events are mental ones. This means that only the language of physical events can articulate the causal laws that bind what happens in our brains to what happens in the rest of the world. Although we may attribute different "mental" properties to what happens in the mind, the substance of the mind must be identical with that of the brain and of other material things if we want to account for how the mind interacts with other objects. Because Davidson recognizes only one substance in the universe, then, he calls his account of the mind ontologically monistic.

Yet do we not every day talk about some idea causing us to run around in some way? Does Davidson want to prohibit us from speaking about thoughts and other mental events causing nonmental events, or to degrade such speech? Not at all. He simply wants us to respect as well a second condition which defines how we should understand the causal relations between events in these different languages: although the causal relations between physical events are, in the last analysis, nomological, lawlike, those between mental events and between mental and physical events cannot accommodate such laws. The reason they cannot is as follows. For the language of mental events to comprise more than a private code—and Wittgenstein has demonstrated that it must[30]—it should be capable not only of describing one's own mental events, but also of *ascribing* such events to others. Davidson argues that the latter is possible only if we charitably suppose that these others are more like ourselves than unlike, that they share most of our beliefs and desires. We need to postulate enough of a common backdrop of familiar behavior in order that the others' differences from us, no matter how various and extreme, may at least make sense as *divergences* from aspects by which they otherwise resemble us. Governing this supposition, however, is no mechanical law, but a normative decision to recognize certain features of the others' mental events and the physical events that proceed from them (that is, intentional actions) to be like our own, based on our standards of coherence, rationality, and so on—which ones we so recognize, though, is up to us. This decision, moreover, can always be revised in the light of additional considerations. Consequently, although Davidson considers acts of the brain to be physical events governed by the causal laws that rule over all events in the universe, he acknowledges that when we consider such acts *qua* events in the mind, we cannot reduce our normative, open-ended interpretation of others, which enables us to determine their mental events as such, to an instance of mechanical causation. There is no reason why we should not continue to talk about mental events causing other mental or physical events, but such talk must leave the nature of these causal relations in shadow. Because of this, then, Davidson calls his account of how mind and body are related "anomalous."

When Rorty talks in the same breath about redescribing oneself and making up one's own mind, then, he is talking Davidsonian "mentalese." Put another way, he is talking about the self as being composed of mental events (and of intentional actions caused by mental events) rather than as a chain of physical events (including those in the brain). This is not to say, however, that the self is *not*, *sans phrase*, such a chain—for that would be false—but only that, for the purpose of redescribing oneself, it is more useful to talk about the self in mentalese, even as "physicalese" would be more useful for predicting or controlling behavior. Mentalese employs terms that stress one's own anomalous originality, and that downplay one's subjection to conventional or natural law. When bolstered by metaphorical, poetic experimentation, this language enables us to form a relatively autonomous, fanciful realm for the self to create itself. Thus the self, as a mental being, is a being made up of mentalistic words rather than mind-stuff.

With this response to our second set of questions about the link between self-creation and self-redescription under our belt, we can wrap up our elucidation of Rorty's conception of edification by turning to our last set, which asks about why Rorty considers activities that enable us to "tell a story about one's causes in a new language" to be more important than more materialistic events that remake us as well. The reason why harks back to one of the overarching purposes of the Rortyan self: to overcome the fear of death. As discussed above, edifying linguistic activities enhance our sense of ourselves as mental beings; they thus differ from activities such as eating, drinking, and earning more, which tend to defer to our physical being. These two aspects of us, once again, are compatible, but by putting his money on the redescriptive powers of the mind, Rorty attempts to loosen (not break) the hold on our selves of our bodies, without whitewashing those anomalies that compose our selves in Platonic universalisms. He wants to protect our individualities both from physical and, in a sense, metaphysical death. His sense of selfhood, of personhood, is in the end based on a Nietzschean vision of how to redeem one's past, mortified as fateful fact, *dramatically* as an aesthetic achievement. This vision of how to overcome death is contrasted with the Platonic quest for the True World as follows:

> The drama of an individual human life, or of the history of humanity as a whole, is not one in which a preexistent goal is triumphantly reached or tragically not reached. Neither a constant external reality nor an unfailing interior source of inspiration forms a background

for such dramas. Instead, to see one's life, or the life of one's community, as a dramatic narrative is to see it as a process of Nietzschean self-overcoming. The paradigm of such a narrative is the life of the genius who can say of the relevant portion of the past, "Thus I willed it," because she has found a way to describe that past which the past never knew, and thereby found a self to be which her precursors never knew was possible.[31]

Will you be able to recast what life throws, and has thrown, at you in your own terms?—that is the question. To the extent that each one of us has rewritten our lives in this way, overcoming the just-the-facts narratives that our precursors put us in, to the extent that, in so remaking ourselves, we leave a mark on the language (and effective history) shared by our community, each of us can celebrate as we go a *history* of *original decisions*, however constrained, whose *significance* cannot be cancelled by the death of our *bodies*. In such a history, those events that affect our bodies and surroundings, while certainly liable to have a great deal of importance *attached* to them, cannot be as important as the edifying events that enable us to attach importance to anything, the events that enable us to place chains of causes and effects in a meaningful context. For, deprived of such a context, our bodies will simply tend to adapt to the vicissitudes of our health and finances until they can do so no longer, whereupon they will break down, without incident, "absurdly."

(What I would want to stress, and probably Rorty would too, is that such Nietzschean narratives are more important to us *for the purposes of edification*. For the purposes of building a community, of reinforcing our sense of solidarity, on the contrary, it may be more important to converse in a more materialistic language. The reason for this is that the controllable causes of suffering stand out less mystifyingly when they are described as physical events affecting our bodies. I venture an argument for this view in the next chapter.)

Thus the problem of personhood, for Rorty, boils down not to the question, How does our consciousness essentially differentiate us from animals and reveal what part of us will survive animal death? but rather to, What sort of human self do I want to make of my animal life to leave death with? Rorty calls the lifelong project called forth by this latter question "edification": another name for it would be "autobiography." As we edify ourselves in response to events that befall us—including childhood traumas, what history teachers tell us, love letters we struggle to compose, medical tests we suffer, chance chats, and so forth—we develop our ability to weave contingent but consistent stories of the course of our own lives. Each autobiography, in this sense, functions like a type of Davidsonian language, spinning "centerless networks of beliefs and desires [whose] vocabularies and opinions are determined by historical circumstance," that is, historical accident.[32] They give our humanity a new sense.

> By seeing every human being as consciously or unconsciously acting out an idiosyncratic fantasy, we can see the distinctively human, as opposed to animal, portion of each human life as the use for symbolic purposes of every particular person, object, situation, event, and word encountered in later life.[33]

Yet unlike the way we normally read such autobiographies, where we take it that the subject and narrator of the tale, though identical, exist at different times outside of the tale, Rorty argues that the self of the tale *is* the tale itself. For him, autobiography is not one optional project among many that the self can engage in, but rather constitutes the very means by which, and the medium in which, the self forms itself; it is a necessary condition for the self to exist. This expanded idea of autobiography becomes easier to grasp when we see how it can elucidate the Kantian notion that the subject transcends the mechanical world, without tying that notion to Kant's account of mental synthesis. Kant held that our various experiences at different times are unified by a subject that transcends the empirical order of things which that subject constitutes. This means that this subject or self also transcends, and remains distinct from, the empirical self, which at any moment, in any of its incarnations, could be an object of experience for that subject. Without such a transcendence there would be no self. Does it follow, then, that we are split into transcendental and empirical selves, that half of us, so to speak, is an object that is represented in the world, and so buffeted about and marked by events giving us sensible intuitions, while the other half is an other-worldly, representing subject that stays essentially the same and so without history, possessing only *a priori* concepts of understanding? Rorty suggests not, because both of these selves would amount to things that must be either inside or outside the world. Rorty's notion of the self, in contrast, like Wittgenstein's, is "a limit of the world."[34] For Wittgenstein, the self is not a thing that one can point to, but more like a condition for there to be anything at all.

> If I wrote a book called *The World as I Found It*, I should have to include a report on my body, and should have to say which parts were subordinate to my will, and which were not, etc., this being a method of isolating the subject, or rather of showing that in an important sense there is no subject; for it alone could *not* be mentioned in that book.[35]

Nevertheless, it does make sense to write about this world as belonging to *me*. "The world is *my* world: this is manifest in the fact that the limits of *language* (of that language which alone I understand) mean the limits of *my* world."[36] Because the world must appear in language in order to appear at all, it must appear to the self that understands that this language forms a world, and it cannot appear to a self that does not understand this language. The self, accordingly, manifests its character in the writing of such a book; for Rorty, however, this implies that the title should be changed from *The World as I Found It: Reflections of a Mirroring Consciousness*, to *The World as I Created It: The Self as Writing Machine*. And presumably the argument of this chapter, with its speculative attempts to redescribe the Cartesian notion of our personhood, would comprise an apt introduction to such a book. Finally, what would make the book something special, something to take pride in at the moment of death, is that it would contain unique features.

For the writer of that book and the weaver of that self, "maturity"—a definitive virtue of the Enlightenment according to Kant[37]—now amounts to "an ability to seek out new redescriptions of one's own past—an ability to take a nominalistic, ironic, view of oneself."[38] In this sense, maturity is what an edifying education should foster.

Rorty opposes this "aesthetic search for self-enlargement" to the "ascetic search for purity" and for authenticity:

> The desire to purify oneself is the desire to slim down, to peel away everything that is accidental, to will one thing, to intensify, to become a simpler and more transparent being. The desire to enlarge oneself is the desire to embrace more and more possibilities, to be constantly learning, to give oneself over entirely to curiosity, to end by having envisaged all the possibilities of the past and of the future. [39]

As our selves enlarge and our vocabulary of self-descriptions grows, we become increasingly "playful, free, and inventive in our choice of self-descriptions."[40] We pick up the knack of juggling, on the one hand, the sense that our selves are up to each of us to redescribe, with, on the other hand, the sense that the self is never any *thing* that we can fix in an autobiographically descriptive text—with, as the third torch up in the air, the admission that influencing all this are causal forces that are only partially under control. Sweating through this game helps "slough off the idea that we have a true self, one shared with all other humans," an idea which we still might find tempting if we were engaged in purifying ourselves.[41] Maturity accordingly ceases to be based on self-knowledge, and instead becomes a matter of achieved self-creation.

It is hard to see how Rorty could reject any more explicitly the tradition of metaphysics and "moral perfectionism" with which we opened the book. Do we now have sufficient reason to conclude that the desire for liberal education should not be metaphysical, that we should not engage in such an education out of a love of perfection? If Rorty's argument holds up, yes. But in the next chapter, I shall point out some serious problems with the arguments, problems rooted in the implications of the argument for how we can cope with cultural conflict.

To round out this exposition of Rorty's notion of personhood, we need to turn to one last question. How do I prevent my project of self-creation, for instance, from colliding with and destroying yours? It is precisely because we can no longer rely on accounts of human nature to stipulate where each one of us stands with respect to others, that conversation becomes indispensable in order to prevent self-enlargement from becoming self-imperialism. Along with the notion of the true self has gone the notion of a preestablished harmony between selves; whatever harmony we need to accommodate prudently our individual edifying activities to those of others must now be hammered out by human hands. This is why, then, Rorty's new conception of selfhood dovetails nicely with that of conversational reason for ethical solidarity. Rorty seals this marriage when he closes *Philosophy and the Mirror of Nature* as follows:

> The only point on which I would insist is that philosophers' moral concern should be with continuing the conversation of the West, rather than with insisting upon a place for the traditional problems of modern philosophy within that conversation.[42]

Where are we finally, then, with respect to those problems? In the last chapter, we examined how Rorty reformulated the problem of reason so as to detach it from the problem of consciousness; this chapter correspondingly recounts how he reformulated the problem of personhood so as likewise to detach it from that of consciousness, and to fit it to that of reason. These two chapters, then, leave the old epistemological problem of consciousness to wither away, and equip us with a new, conversational conception of our reason and a new, edifying conception of our selfhood. Rorty's arguments against an epistemological education for cultural reform, therefore, end up being arguments for an alternative education that would help us become more conversational and edifying beings, and would encourage us to reform our culture so that it promotes the welfare of such beings. His arguments broach an alternative conception of the desire for liberal education.

What remains to be seen, though, is whether this desire for liberal education is not too compromised by its connection to destructive tendencies in the Nietzschean will to power. As we noted in the last chapter, Rorty's notion of reason entails that true sentences articulating beliefs and values are to be actively asserted rather than discovered; this appears to give the green light to a Nietzschean subject who would will, with or without conversation, "it shall become thus and thus." Our suspicions are now further strengthened in this chapter, where Rorty explicitly gives his blessing to a Nietzschean conception of selfhood, such that the self, instead of discovering her or his place in the true world, "organizes a portion of an otherwise meaningless world oneself." Having taken on board such Nietzschean sentiments, how can Rorty's work possibly transport us not only out of the epistemological picture of philosophy, culture, and liberal education, but also beyond the frame of nihilism?

5

CONVERSATIONAL EDIFICATION, LIBERALISM, AND CULTURAL ANTAGONISM

So far we have recounted how Rorty's arguments enable us to opt out of the Cartesian equation of the problems of reason and of personhood with that of consciousness; his arguments demonstrate how we may address the former two problems while ignoring the latter. They pave the way for transforming liberal education from an epistemological education for cultural reform, one that would promote the role of metaphysics, to an education that aspires to reform culture by promoting in it the powers of conversation and edification. Coordinating these powers, we may consolidate them into a single expression of *conversational edification:* by this term I mean *the power to converse reasonably with others for the purpose of edifying oneself.* In this chapter, I shall first explain how a liberal education guided by the desire to foster this power in the members of a culture, may be distinguished from one guided by metaphysical desire. I shall then turn to a problem with the former desire, however, which Rorty's liberalism appears unable to solve.

Any education that promotes liberal learning, let alone the power of conversational edification, is bound to evoke the legend of Socrates; we saw this earlier in our discussion of Oakeshott. Yet the Socratic example is, of course, traditionally linked to the Platonic longing for metaphysics; hence philosophers of education who have been interested in Socratic education, like Hutchins and Allan Bloom, tend to take metaphysics seriously as well. Since Rorty, like Dewey, finds the whole temptation to metaphysics problematic, he can only appeal to the Socratic example if he disjoins it from its Platonic interpretation. He accomplishes this, in a passage I cited earlier, by redescribing the moral of Socrates' life:

> What matters to us [pragmatist] "intellectuals," as opposed to the [metaphysical] "philosopher," is the imaginativeness and openness of discourse, not proximity to something lying beyond discourse. Both Platonists and Deweyans take Socrates as their hero. For Plato, the life of Socrates did not make sense unless there was something like the Idea of the Good at the end of the dialectical road. For Dewey, the life of Socrates made sense as a symbol of a life of openness and curiosity. It was an experimental life—the sort of life that is encouraged by, and in turn encourages, the American democratic experiment.[1]

What Rorty offers us here is less a summary portrait of Socrates than an imaginative variation on one of the themes of his life: that is, his habit of engaging others in dialectical conversation. Platonists understand the desire for such conversation to be a longing to acquire metaphysical knowledge of the Good. Rorty understands this desire to be experimental curiosity, curiosity about possibilities for self-redescription and edification, and about how these possibilities may be extended to more people through democratic cultural reform.[2] Such curiosity has little interest in the idea of the Good for its own sake, or in a philosophy that would set the standards for the good of the culture as a whole.

This idea of Socratic conversational edification entails a shift in how we understand not only the desire that leads to such conversation but also what the conversation will turn on, what will be its pivotal content. The claims of metaphysics are replaced by those which suggest how certain beliefs and desires rooted in the culture you inherit may be refashioned in conversation in certain edifying ways. According to this understanding, a culture is composed not of knowledge-claims grounded on epistemologically foundational, metaphysical truths, but of a reasonably pragmatic system of linguistic tools that speakers may use to redescribe themselves, collectively and individually. The meaning of "we" and of "I" are the stakes of Socratic liberal learning.

For the purposes of such conversational edification, the resources that foreign cultures have to offer become especially useful. Indeed, Rorty elucidates the shift in the pivotal content of this liberal learning by contrasting the value that Allan Bloom, Hutchins's successor, and that Dewey ascribe to the exploration of other cultures in education. Bloom interprets Plato's allegory that we are imprisoned in a cave of deceptive shadows as follows:

> A culture is a cave. He [Plato] did not suggest going around to other cultures as a solution to the limitations of the cave. Nature should be the standard by which we judge our lives and the lives of peoples. That is why philosophy, not history or anthropology, is the most important human science. Only dogmatic assurance that thought is culture-bound, that there is no nature, is what makes our educators so certain that the only way to escape the limitations of our time and place is to study other cultures.[3]

Contrariwise, Rorty observes that:

> Dewey did suggest going around to other cultures. He thought that the benefit of going around (via history and anthropology) to other cultures was the same as that offered by the arts—the enlargement of our moral imaginations. He put his faith in the arts rather than in philosophy because he did not believe that there was such a thing as "nature" to serve as "the standard." The idea of "human nature," like "the quest for certainty," was a cowardly attempt to reduce a self-creating being to one that was already finished and unchangeable.[4]

Needless to say, Rorty sides with Dewey. He supports Socratic conversation that could enlarge our imaginations by confronting us with other cultural alternatives, by inviting us to redescribe ourselves in the face of unfamiliar possibilities. He encourages us to explore other "caves"—only he would likely drop the whole cave metaphor, which suggests that there is another realm of nature closer to the metaphysical sun, and replace it with the image of humanly constructed, humanly inhabited, culturally divergent palaces. A culture, then, is defined by its differences from other cultures, not by any difference from nature; the former differences, moreover, are to be appreciated for their edifying possibilities. Furthermore, he could reply to Bloom's charge that such a cultural education is based on "dogmatic assurance" by rolling up his antiepistemological arguments, which destroy the grounds of any claims to metaphysical truth, and so turn the charge back on Bloom. He could further cast in a dubious light the very impulse to metaphysics by redescribing it as Nietzschean resentment, a hindrance to our democratic experiment in the cultivation of self-creation through the toleration and appreciation of edifying difference.

In the spirit of this experiment, when you exercise your freedom to struggle to solve, rather than meekly accept, problems in your culture, you are engaged in a project that is heroic. This project may lead you to give your life to the development of those conversationally edifying powers latent in your culture and in its neighbors. Out of the development of such resources may emerge a better culture that lacks the old limitations.

To appreciate such heroism so that it calls forth the same impulses in ourselves is for Rorty the aim of general education, or what I would call liberal learning. From such learning:

> . . . we will not get instructions about what to do, but rather models of the sort of virtue which we must exemplify. . . . None of these will be accounts of man's encounter with Reality or with Truth, but all of them will be accounts of man's attempt to solve problems, to work out the potentialities of the languages and activities available to them. In the course of such attempts we encounter heroes who created new languages, and thus new genres, new disciplines, and new societies. These heroes of humanity are the people who dissolved the problems of their day by transcending the vocabulary in which these problems were posed.
>   . . . [We should] give students a chance for intellectual hero-worship by letting them see intellectual greatness as greatness in solving problems.[5]

Rorty invites us to heroicize those people who exemplify the virtuous power of conversational edification in a culture. Taking a cue from Alfred North Whitehead, Rorty associates the worship of such heroes, and the exercise of conversational edification which that worship promotes, with the Romance stage of learning appropriate to general education:

> "General Studies" is a catchword for the sort of education which aims at Romance. The fear that education may become merely "vo-

cational" and no longer "liberal" is the fear that the student will never have heroes, will never fall in love with anything. . . . The sense of the human community which seems to me the goal of education requires that one avoid both a cold-hearted, and self-absorbed, relativism and the complacent sense that only those who have fallen in love with certain particular heroes are fit companions. There is a difference between the sort of love affair which is merely obsessional and the sort which frees one to love all other lovers, even those whose loves are centered on objects whose attractions one cannot understand. It is this second sort of romance which one hopes general education will produce.

The goal of general studies seems to me to make sure that no student has only *one* hero, and that there is enough overlap between the students' *sets* of heroes to permit the students to share their romantic sensibilities, to have interesting conversations with one another. The aim of such conversations is, once again, not to seek the Truth but just to bind us together.[6]

What Rorty, as opposed to Plato or Allan Bloom, means by eros in liberal learning should now be clear. It is the attraction we feel for those engaged in heroically solving the problems of their cultures by developing the resources in those cultures of conversational edification, using the resources of other cultures as well. This attraction inspires us to emulate such heroes, to respect those who have dedicated themselves to different heroes, and to hold edifying conversations with as many different kinds of hero-worshippers as possible. Eros is thus a longing to participate in a life where such problem-solving, such cultural reform, is the point of living. It is a longing which general education should foster.

Teaching general studies (the last years of high school or the first year of college—the stage of Romance)—is erotic or nothing. Either the student is moved to think of himself as a potential member of a community which includes both his teacher and the author of the book being read, or nothing happens at all.[7]

For the most part, I find Rorty's conception of Socratic conversational edification convincing. I believe that he has posed a successful challenge to Allan Bloom's and Hutchins's calls for a metaphysical education by reinforcing the Deweyan suspicion that such an education presumes an authoritarian conception of knowledge dangerous for a society that would be liberal and democratic. He furthermore links this suspicion to our growing recognition of our cultural diversity. He supplements arguments for multiculturalist education that stress the need to protect cultures from monocultural hegemony— from, in Bloom's case, a liberal education whose preoccupation with distinguishing natural truth from cultural opinion is rooted in European culture alone—with an argument that a multiculturalist education could help all in it to develop their sense of selfhood. He invites us to elaborate the goals and processes of a multiculturalist liberal learning in response to a new sense of what could motivate that learning: the longing to revitalize heroically, in the face of concrete problems, your culture's power of conversational edification.

Before we respond to this invitation, though, we need to confront a doubt lurking in the wings. Inasmuch as the Rortyan self who seeks to edify herself or himself in conversation resembles the Nietzschean subject who willfully values some desires and devalues others, has not Rorty burdened us with enough Nietzschean baggage to mire us in nihilism? Another way of putting this is as the worry that the self's quest to edify itself can only flourish at the expense of efforts to negotiate a conversational consensus, one which would promote values in the name of a culture and not just of an individual. Would I not, for example, be ready to affirm my desire for, be ready to value, actions and things that distinguish me from others, and conversely be willing to devalue actions and things that liken me to others participating in a common cause? The conversational reason that would issue in a basis for our values, and the edifying self that would create my own values, seem bound to clash, rendering "conversational edification" a contradiction in terms.

This is a serious challenge to any Rortyan philosophy of liberal education. Rorty recognizes this, and he elaborates a historicist liberalism that he believes could defuse the challenge. I find his response helpful, but I shall argue that it ultimately fails to curb the Nietzschean tendency of his pragmatism to perpetuate cultural antagonism. This failure suggests that we need to think more deeply about the public realm we want such an education to foster, and about what kind of educational discourse is appropriate to such a realm.

Rorty's response to the challenge takes the form of an attempt to liberalize the edifying self. The need for this becomes apparent when we examine in more detail that self's nominalistic and ironic attitude to how things and events of that one's self and world are described. Such an attitude, as we saw in the last chapter, distances one from those descriptions, and gives one elbowroom to exercise one's experimental curiosity in redescribing oneself and one's world in one's own, new terms. If one did not adopt such an attitude, one would be more inclined to hold on to given descriptions and less inclined to edify oneself.

This attitude may be analyzed into three components. The first consists of the language by which we relate things and events to ourselves, the language of our autobiography:

> All human beings carry about a set of words which they employ to justify their actions, their beliefs, and their lives. These are the words in which we formulate praise of our friends and contempt for our enemies, our long-term projects, our deepest self-doubts and our highest hopes. They are the words in which we tell, sometimes prospectively and sometimes retrospectively, the story of our lives. I shall call these words a person's "final vocabulary."[8]

Now suppose it dawns on you that your final vocabulary cannot be "final," because it is merely *a vocabulary*. This nominalistic realization, and how it affects ironically the self of that vocabulary, make up the second and central element of the attitude:

> I shall define an "ironist" as someone who fulfills three conditions: (1) She has radical and continuing doubts about the final vocabulary she currently uses, because she has been impressed by other vocabularies, vocabularies taken as final by people or books she has encountered; (2) she realizes that argument phrased in her present vocabulary can neither underwrite nor dissolve these doubts; (3) insofar as she philosophizes about her situation, she does not think that her vocabulary is closer to reality than others, that it is in touch with a power not herself.
> I call people of this sort "ironists" because their realization that

> anything can be made to look good or bad by being redescribed, and their renunciation of the attempt to formulate criteria of choice between final vocabularies, puts them in the position which Sartre called "meta-stable": never quite able to take themselves seriously because always aware that the terms in which they describe themselves are subject to change, always aware of the contingency and fragility of their final vocabularies, and thus of their lives.[9]

Such a realization may be triggered, of course, by the antiepistemological arguments of the past three chapters.

The last element of the attitude of "ironism" that Rorty proceeds to define is its dialectical antithesis, expressed by those who would consider an ironic overturning of their final vocabularies to be an unequivocal disaster, one that destroys their very identities. Such a person might take to strengthening, extending, and even enforcing that vocabulary. She or he could do that by claiming that the vocabulary is grounded on epistemologically fundamental truths— or on the conversational consensus, the we-intentions, of her or his culture.

> The opposite of irony is common sense. For that is the watchword of those who unself-consciously describe everything important in terms of the final vocabulary to which they and those around them are habituated. To be commonsensical is to take for granted that statements formulated in that final vocabulary suffice to describe and judge the beliefs, actions and lives of those who employ alternative final vocabularies.[10]

What these definitions posit, then, is the existence of two kinds of characters or selves, distinguished by contrasting attitudes toward their final vocabularies: the ironist and the "commonsensicalist." Between these two characters there is tension and the potential for conflict; they incarnate, as it were, the latent antagonism between the communal values of conversation and the individualistic ones of edification. This becomes clear if we imagine them starting up a conversation somewhere, say at a bus stop. Warmly, the commonsensicalist brings up a topic from his, let us imagine, Christian final vocabulary that he is dying to talk about, hoping to profit from an edifying exchange of views with his fellow worshiper. What a shock he suffers when he learns that the ironist does not take his religious concerns seriously at all! His dismay grows as the ironist, politely, yet with overpowering persuasiveness, makes it clear that not only does she have no use for Christian concerns, but that she has good reason to suspect them of deadening our sense of life's sacredness. By the end of the conversation-turned-dispute, the commonsensicalist feels as if he has been left choking in the dust, seething with resentment that his values have been trampled on, but unable to utter an unanticipated word in reply.

We might describe the moral of such an encounter as follows:

> Consider what happens when a child's precious possessions—the little things around which he weaves fantasies that make him a little different from all other children—are redescribed as "trash" and thrown away. Or consider what happens when these possessions are made to look ridiculous alongside the possessions of another, richer child. . . . The redescribing ironist, by threatening one's final vocabulary, and thus one's ability to make sense of oneself in one's own terms rather than hers, suggests that one's self and one's world are futile, obsolete, *powerless*. Redescription often humiliates.[11]

Irony can be an arm for bullying those who lastingly value their final vocabularies. And in the case where the final vocabulary under attack is one which a culture shares—a commonsensical final vocabulary—the ironist, the edifying self, stands to appear a hostile, destructive figure. Indeed Rorty acknowledges as much: "I cannot go on to claim that there could or ought to be a culture whose public rhetoric is *ironist*."[12]

How, then, can we protect our public, conversational discourse about shared values (we-intentions) from irony's incendiary touch? One solution would be to eschew irony altogether, and to argue that we ought to restrict ourselves to being commonsensicalists. Another solution would be to look for some deeper realm of human experience from which both ironic edification and conversational common sense proceed, and in which they may be somehow synthesized. Rorty declines both of these responses because they end up appealing, in his view, to a Platonic notion of human nature which he has already criticized. Both claim that there is some fundamental way of describing human experience which precludes ironic redescription, and which allows us either to rule out irony or to synthesize it, in a stable (nonironic) manner, with common sense.

The alternative solution Rorty puts forward is not to reconcile irony and common sense in some theory of human nature, but to compromise between these two attitudes and the activities they inspire in practice. He calls us to respect a division between the public and private realms; this allows him to restrict the edifying, and other, effects of irony to our private lives, while maintaining our public commitment to the results of conversational reason. In taking this line, he joins a liberal tradition of thinkers who, like J.S. Mill, are centrally concerned about defending a conception of negative freedom. His work construes the political task of reforming one's society as one of striking a fair and just balance between our private desires and public responsibilities. Thus the edifying effects of irony would enter on one side of the scale; on the other would enter irony's potential damage to others, and the necessity, therefore, to listen to the other with sincere sensitivity.

> For my private purposes, I may redescribe you and everybody else in terms which have nothing to do with my attitude toward your actual or possible suffering. My private purposes, and that part of my final vocabulary which is not relevant to my public actions, are none of your business. But as I am a liberal, the part of my final vocabulary which is relevant to such actions requires me to become aware of all the various ways in which other human beings whom I might act on can be humiliated. So the liberal ironist needs as much imaginative acquaintance with alternative final vocabularies as possible, not just for her own edification, but in order to understand the actual and possible humiliation of the people who use these alternative final vocabularies.[13]

This passage points to another reason why liberal learning, that is, conversational edification, should be multicultural. We need to learn how to recognize the "actual and possible humiliation" of members of such cultures so that we may ethically avoid contributing to it.

We may be skeptical, however, that left to their own devices, our ironic proclivities could police themselves. As each of us exercises irony on ourselves, would not such wit spill over to, invade, and disrupt the final vocabularies of our familiars? And if such disruption spread to our consensual institutions, then liberal values might lose their credibility in a society threatened by discord, such that the liberal reconciliation of private irony and public responsibility no longer appears to be an option when there is a demand to choose sides in a conflict. (Thomas Mann, in *Doctor Faustus*, describes such a disruption in the intellectual circle which forms around Leverkühn, and which presages the Nazi destruction of democratic institutions.)[14] What we evidently require, therefore, is some way to limit rationally the realm of irony. Beyond a certain point, it should be possible to claim, we ought to stop waxing ironic, and start extending to our interlocutor more liberal consideration— on pain of being stigmatized an irrationalist.

To the disappointment of those who would make the above scruple a first principle of rational criticism, such as Jürgen Habermas, Rorty maintains that as long as we do not want to relapse into metaphysics and its attendant epistemology, this way of clamping down on our ironic tongue cannot be in the offing.[15] He notes that no ironist can rely on a "reason to care about suffering," for any such reason would have to be phrased in a vocabulary that is open to transformation. All that the ironist who would be liberal has got to fall back on:

> . . . is not finding such a reason but making sure that she notices suffering when it occurs. Her hope is that she will not be limited by her own final vocabulary when faced with the possibility of humiliating someone with a quite different final vocabulary.[16]

Where does this hope come from? Apparently it belongs to a larger hope or desire that she carries, one which is tied to a belief about the nature of her solidarity with the whole human race:

> She [the ironist] thinks that what unites her with the rest of the species is not a common language but just susceptibility to pain and in particular to that special sort of pain which the brutes do not share with the humans—humiliation. On her conception, human solidarity is not a matter of sharing a common truth or a common goal but of sharing a common selfish hope, the hope that one's world—

the little things around which one has woven into one's final vocabulary—will not be destroyed.[17]

In other words, what binds us together is not some sophisticated version of common sense, but simply our prelinguistic, animalistic vulnerability to pain, extending into our linguistic behavior. Recognizing or believing this evidently prompts, then, the hopeful desire in the ironist to avoid the pain of having her final vocabulary, and the world it composes, destroyed.

But why should anyone believe this? And even if there are good reasons for this belief that all of us share a common vulnerability, why should it and its associated desire cause me to care about *others*? As long as I am safe, why should another's suffering cause me any grief?

One way that Rorty could start to respond to this wave of questions is to argue that we cannot sincerely doubt that we care about anyone at all. In the grip of such skeptical doubt, we become absentmindedly blind to concrete facts in our personal histories; once we take another look at these facts, however, we may realize that they are more important to us than any need to doubt them so. *Of course* we each care about *some* people (or a quasi-person like a pet). Any discourse that asks us to deny this cherished fact has to appeal to something for which we care at least as much; the only thing that can move us to revise a belief and desire is another belief and desire. Are there beliefs and desires unconnected with particular persons that matter to us more than the people we love? Certainly much feminist thought, as exemplified in Nel Noddings's *Caring*, would suggest otherwise.[18] For this reason, then, Rorty would likely contend that the real, pragmatic question we should be considering is why we do not care about *this* person and her or his kind.

This question is one about our own and this person's particular history, about the historical circumstances that divide us from them. The key is to see that any such history may be also redescribed. The stranger can always be made, through redescription, to look less like a Martian and more like your grandfather. When this happens, reasons to care become superfluous; *by definition* you care about your grandfather or other beloved figure. This is why, then, Rorty puts his money on what he calls "noticing suffering" and an "imaginative acquaintance with alternative final vocabularies" (and on what Rousseau and Shelley called the "moral imagination"). These concepts serve as shorthand for the process of learning to understand another's history sympathetically, such that you notice how similar that person's world is to your own or to someone you are close to, and you feel how moving their actual or potential suffering is.

Might there not be cases, however, where the other's world is so alien to us that to redescribe it in our terms is to misdescribe it? Or even worse, to do it an injustice? This is the notorious problem of incommensurable worldviews or languages, originally formulated by Thomas S. Kuhn, Paul Feyerabend, and other philosophers of science, and elaborated by Jean-François Lyotard to bear on all areas of social life.[19] It is more precisely a problem of justification: How can you reasonably judge which of two descriptions of a phenomenon is true if one or the other of those descriptions employ terms which, when translated into the (paradigmatic) language of the alternative description, already bias the issue in favor of that alternative description?

As an example of this problem, consider again the debate in Chapter Two between Terran philosophers and their Antipodean counterparts, their "cultural Other." Let us imagine that the Terrans decide to stop worrying about whether the Antipodean talk of neural states is really about mental states, and to get on instead with converting the Antipodeans to our better way of talking. In this unlikely event, we might see exchanges like this one.

> TERRAN: Look, tell me what you're feeling now, I mean, what state you're having.
> ANTIPODEAN: Well as long as you insist, I'm having M–19!
> TERRAN: (Looks up M–19 in the dictionary.) Ah, you're feeling mad. You're feeling what we would call "mad." Now, don't you see, the term "mad," with its overtones of "madness," is a much

more emotional, more expressive, richer term than your impossibly clinical "M–19."

However crude the example, we can sense the dilemma looming on the horizon. When the Terran translates "M–19" into "mad," he is apt to believe that there is a gain in useful meaning, and correspondingly to believe that meaning is lost when one reverses the translation. He might therefore try to introduce this gain as evidence for the superiority of Terran over Antipodean descriptions of "mental phenomena." But the last term betrays a bias that is already built into this translation: namely the *social* purposes that *we* bring to bear on what occurs in our minds. In contrast, after the Antipodean has cooled down, she might rejoin as follows:

> ANTIPODEAN: Well tell me then, if one feels "mad," what will one feel next?
> TERRAN: I suppose that depends on one's personality, and on incidental factors like the weather.
> ANTIPODEAN: And what if one has "M–19;" what neural state, all things being equal, *must* come next? Go ahead, look it up.
> TERRAN: M–20.
> ANTIPODEAN: I rest my case!

We Terrans may feel baffled by the Antipodean's note of triumph, thinking to ourselves "so what?" Yet to a culture that prizes the prediction and control of what goes on in our brains, the knowledge of what brain state will occur next may seem like an indisputable, natural criterion for judging which term describes the phenomenon in question better. Such a criterion thus appears just as valid as the Terran's appeal to our expressive purposes.

The problem of incommensurability, then, is that there are no neutral criteria for judging which is the better descriptive term; each term under consideration implies a whole language, including the cultural purposes for which that language is used, that begs the question of what is to count as a better description. To have access to neutral criteria, we would have to transcend both languages in question, and arrive at Nature's Own Language to which they both approximate. We would have to appeal to a Platonic, metaphysical conception of intergalactic order. But as we have remarked repeatedly, Rorty wants to insist that we perceive and speak about the world only from inside our particular contingent circumstances, including our own *specific* linguistic inheritance. When we try to judge between different descriptions, all that we can do is to relate, from our perspective, what others call true to what we call true, or, bluntly put, to what *is* true; "Nature" has no independent say in the matter. This means that we try to translate as many of the sentences that others hold true as we can into sentences that we hold true, and accept the fact that we will have to consider the remainder either false or meaningless *to us*.

But if this is the case, then do not all our judgments amount merely to relativistic preferences, since both descriptions and languages are valid in their own terms? Do we not even have to admit that, in some sense, Terrans and Antipodeans inhabit completely separate universes that cannot be neutrally measured against each other or compared? How dare we, then, consider redescribing Antipodeans in our parochial terms, even for the purposes of sympathizing with them.

This conclusion would severely narrow our capacity to notice suffering and to expand our moral imaginations. It would render Rorty's attempt to liberalize the edifying self without appealing to a reason to care too ethnocentrically ineffectual. We can avoid it, however, if we initially acknowledge that what does make us Terrans care about how Antipodeans look at things is some interest that we have; without that interest, the Antipodeans just would not have anything significant to say to us. (And of course this, and what follows, holds the other way around for the Antipodeans.) Therefore it is desirable for us to contrive a way to translate Antipodean utterances into terms that make a difference to us, irrespective, ultimately, of whether the Antipodeans themselves would endorse these translations. Our cultural language, with the interests that it carries, is the yardstick that comes first.

But the story hardly ends there. What prevents the violence that we Terrans do to Antipodean beliefs and meanings from *necessarily* making a mockery of the dialogue is that the more Antipodean sentences we can translate into our language, however roughly, the more of our sentences we can translate into their language. As this exchange expands, while specific infelicities in specific translations may remain unrecognized, the distance separating our prejudices and preconceptions as a whole from those of the Antipodeans—Gadamer's hermeneutic distance—becomes more and more unmistakable. Our faulty, occasionally unjust, self-serving translations gradually enable us not only to understand the Antipodeans, in a fashion, but also to learn to speak their language for ourselves; as a result, an alien language and culture begin to take over, rearrange, and exhibit our own beliefs in surprising ways. Insofar as we can resist the reactionary temptation to stamp out a language that may reveal how deeply prejudiced we are, we may accept an emerging invitation to move from a one-sided criticism of translated Antipodean beliefs to a bilingual, open-ended, critical dialogue with the Antipodeans about our historically different preconceptions, for the purpose of changing them. And why would we Terrans, at least, want to change such preconceptions instead of denying or reasserting them? Because we are interested in edifying ourselves and in preventing the humiliation of others. Thus questions about the commensurability of particular, one-to-one translations cease to make much difference once we appreciate the value of what the Antipodean culture, as a marvelously divergent, coherent whole, has to offer for redescribing ourselves, and how it may be damaged by our disrespect.

Of course on the way to such an appreciation, there are all sorts of practical difficulties that may wreck our effort. As we talk, we may simply decide that the Antipodeans are wrong about everything of any interest to us (for instance, about those sentences that express "higher cognitive content"), and that we are wasting our time. Yet the dialogue need not come to such a stuffy end; with a little more digging, it may emerge that the other has plenty to teach us, and so we may begin to use her or his language to question and adjust our own. Conversely, there is the possibility, which especially bothers Allan Bloom, that we might confuse respect for the other's beliefs with the notion that everything the other says must be just as true as what we say. Again, though, things need not come to such a empty end; we may reach a point where we sincerely affirm that, *were* we in the same circumstances the other is in, we would hold that such-and-such is true—but still maintain that it is better to accept (to refrain from redescribing) the circumstances that we are in, and so maintain that such-and-such is false. And we may care enough about our interlocutor to urge her or him to give our viewpoint, our cultural language, a run for its money, for what it might do for her or him and her or his culture, before rejecting it—without thereby wrapping ourselves in missionary robes. In the end, therefore, the success of the dialogue turns not on precise translations and relativistic dilemmas, but on the goodwill of the interlocutors and on the sincerity of their interests in edification and in the prevention of humiliation. However fuzzy and chancy these qualities may be, there are just no substitutes for them.

Furthermore, it is important to remember that, for the meantime at least, we are concerned here not with Terrans and Antipodeans, but with different human cultures and their histories. When a stranger's particular history seems to defy understanding, it may help to take our bearings from one of the things common to all human beings: the workings of the human body. As we remarked earlier in connection with Davidson's view of the mind, mental events occur alongside physical events that subject our bodies to causal forces and their laws shaping the whole universe. Most of those forces at any given moment will be beyond our control. Hence the significance Rorty ascribes to our susceptibility to pain: our bodies are relatively defenseless against contingencies we can scarcely predict, let alone manage. More to the point, our species-bodies are bound to suffer from the same kind of forces and events in more or less the same way. When we seek to sympathize with the history of someone different from us, we would do well to remember that those differences take place against the background of a common physiology vulnerable to the same environmental forces. Care for our bodies make us all commonsensical ecologists. (This point has been stressed by Sebastiano Timpanaro in his plea for materialist political criticism, and by Foucault in his studies of how the body is disciplined by normalizing powers in society.)[20]

To drive this last fact home, I would like to call the recognition that our bodies are prone to suffer from the same events that cause a stranger's body to suffer an ironic qualification of the ironist's claim to greater autonomy. Traditionally, radical ironists like Socrates, Kierkegaard, Nietzsche, and Derrida have typically taken pains to make it unmistakable that irony, in the last instance, boomerangs back on the ironist, that to press our ironic criticism of a belief to its logical conclusion will eventually require that we ironically criticize in turn the grounds for that criticism, and so forth. In the case at hand here, that criticism goes around and around the following figure-of-eight. Your ironic redescription of your own or another's final vocabulary, proceeding from a mentalist language of beliefs, desires, and intentional actions—cannot fully acknowledge the causal laws and forces that form the physical universe, and so cannot effectively redescribe (but only fail to describe completely) your body and how it is affected by other bodies. Yet as soon as you attempt to describe how events in and around these bodies are significant for certain purposes—you slip back into a vocabulary of intentions that is open for redescription.

As a consequence, the ironist could never, even if she wanted to, redescribe the other's final vocabulary in such a manner as to make it wholly Other. This does not mean that she cannot redescribe it in a manner that humiliates the other person. But if she does humiliate the other, there is no conscience-killer in principle that could stifle the recognition that this person suffers in the same way that she, or her brother, would suffer. Just as she would rather die than humiliate her brother, she may no longer be able to live with herself without making amends. So being an ironist does not commit you by definition, as opposed to by accident or by intent, to being insensitive to another's suffering, for suffering may always be felt as a common bodily experience, and not as somebody else's mental one. Cavell puts this poignantly: "The crucified human body is our best picture of the unacknowledged human soul."[21] It is this insight (which again echos the impact of Foucault's work) that supports Rorty's belief that what we share with our fellow human beings—

what we acknowledge when we acknowledge our humanity—is our vulnerability to pain.

There is no reason in principle, then, that we cannot be *alternatively* edifying ironists and ecological commonsensicalists. The challenge to become capable of cultivating both these identities is thus a practical one of untangling and weighing the shifting demands they each place from moment to moment on our actions. It is one of balancing our interest in edifying our minds by redescribing the vocabularies with which we are involved, with our interest in protecting bodies like ourselves from pain.

As I remarked earlier, Rorty balances these two interests on the dividing line between the public and private realms. Privately, I may cope with the demands of ironic edification and conversational solidarity by balancing them as I see fit. As soon as my balance spills over into actions with harmful or dangerous social consequences, however, it ought to yield to public regulations roughly in the form of: "Whenever one of us is in circumstances C, that person shall balance these things by doing A." Thus the Rortyan solution to potential conflict between our edifying and conversational projects is straightforward: we need to privatize irony about our culture's we-intentions or values, and to sensitize ourselves to the ways that such irony can cause public humiliation. This solution subjects the experiments we perform for our own edification to constraints determined by we-intentions formulated in conversation. These regulative we-intentions traditionally employ the language of rights to further the reformist politics of democratic liberalism; they are designed to allow as many people to pursue as many different edifying projects as possible, in the hope that the multicultural democracy so formed will be one to which we will be gladly loyal. Irony, then, need not threaten our solidarity, even as it threatens, constructively, the ironist's own final vocabulary.

There remain, however, two problems with Rorty's liberal solution.

The first, which many of his critics have pointed out, is that we cannot literally separate the private and public realms. Any form of behavior can be described in such a way as to stress either its private interest or its public consequences. For example, the process whereby you become, in Harold Bloom's terms, a "strong poet"— the process which, for Rorty, is the paradigm of ironic edification— necessarily involves a struggle with a precursor. You develop a sense of self by "strongly misreading" the work of another; in this misreading, you violate, violently, the other's self-presentation. Often you afterwards publicize this misreading in the form of your own self-presentations. Is this any less an act of public humiliation for the fact that the other is usually in no position to complain? Conversely, the act of affirming certain communal values, or we-intentions, is bound to make a difference to the sense of selfhood. How could I, for example, share a concern about images and discourses that glorify the degradation of women, and still take seriously, for the purposes of my edification, artists and writers who resist this concern? It is hard to imagine that my edification could proceed unaffected by my participation in a cultural conversation.

Rorty could deal with this problem by emphasizing that he is not interested in separating the public and private realms on the basis of some literal, naturalistic, absolute boundary. He wants only to determine degrees of separation that emerge in certain circumstances, and which can be respected for certain purposes. His critics have misunderstood him if they think that he conceives of the separation in black-and-white terms, for the purposes of making a point of theoretical principle. The public-private distinction is a pragmatic tool that promises to help us mitigate conflict between individuals and their society. Even if it proves to be rough and fuzzy when contemplated in abstraction, if in using it we are able to iron out certain conflicts, then we have all the reason we need to affirm its significance.

But this raises a second, more serious problem. If the public-private distinction is to be considered a tool, then we need to ask about who is using it. Who determines how the distinction should be applied in particular circumstances to particular people? Assuming that somebody, or some party, determines this, then what about the others in those circumstances who were not able to make such a determination, or who disagree with it. How else can they under-stand this determination of the relation between their sense of self-hood and their cultural participation, except as an act of imposition?

To see this, consider the intractable controversy these days about whether abortion should be legalized. Here the impulse to separate the public and private realms not only fails to advance us toward a solution, it is one of the things that fuels the conflict. One party believes that the separation should be made such that the disposition of the (early) fetus is in the private realm; the other party places that disposition in the public realm. Who is in a neutral position to separate these realms? And yet somebody must, for nature is silent on the issue.

Without the possibility of proceeding from a position of neutrality, the public-private distinction becomes a tool in the service of partial interests—interests which are liable to provoke partial resistance. When we thus recognize that the use of this tool polarizes and divides us, we become subject to an unevadable question: *Whose values?* Whose values does this distinction, and the discourse of we-intentions regulating its use, serve? Who is the "we" that is being appealed to here, and does it include you or me? And with the advent of these questions, more conflict will be generated which the distinction in question will be useless to resolve.

Indeed, the partiality of the public-private distinction betrays a more serious, irreducible partiality at the very heart of the pragmatist conception of reason. When we evaluate a belief or action in terms of practical costs and benefits, this judgment is bound to provoke the question: Beneficial for whom? As we have seen, and as Rorty admits, there is a "Whiggish," ethnocentric, self-interested property to the narratives we have recourse to in pragmatically justifying our beliefs and actions. We—or some other—can always redescribe our history as one which required suppressing the objections of those who had to bear the costs of our benefits, yet which contains the possibility that these repressed voices may return to disrupt our sense of continuity. Haunting Rorty's pragmatic historicism, then, is the vengeful Messiah of Walter Benjamin's "Theses on the Philosophy of History," cited in my second chapter, a figure which symbolizes resistance to the ethnocentric history of a dominant culture in the name of those whom that culture has condemned to oblivion—and who must reclaim a name for themselves in a warring history. Such a figure reminds us of the force in persuasion, and out of the ashes of the distinction between force and persuasion it gives birth to new possibilities for resistance, needing no more justification than the rhetorical question: Why not revolt against what you have suffered?

This partiality at the heart of pragmatism, moreover, affects more than single individuals. Because it affects the justification of beliefs and actions in conversational, public discourse, the question, Beneficial for whom? distinguishes classes of people according to whether or not they are favored by the particular beliefs or actions at issue. These benefits comprise a stake that brings people together and opposes them to their competitors. However much people may be engaged in individual edification, then, they also have an interest in how the partiality of pragmatist reasons, we-intentions, ally them with some parties in opposition to others. The public realm fostered by Rorty's thought forces each of us to identify with some culture struggling with another for hegemony.

When we recognize that our solidarity with a culture, a solidarity that our conversational reason was supposed to foster, is bound to make us antagonistic to some other culture that the partiality of our reason puts us at odds with, it becomes possible to see that, with a little revision, such reason and ironic edification may be compatible after all. Instead of conceiving of ironic edification as a separation of a new self from her or his given society, we may better conceive of it as a separation of someone who is in the process of identifying with a new, perhaps only half-glimpsed utopian culture, of conversationally affirming her or his solidarity with it, from her or his given culture. Edification may thus be understood to be less of an individualizing process—a process that becomes problematic once we can no longer draw a clear line between the public and private realms—and more of an ironically antagonizing process that determines what we do not want to be, with whom we do not want to be associated. It accompanies the process of conversational reason in the same way that attaching yourself to one group may be accompanied by detaching yourself from another, and vice versa. Together, both processes lead you to affirm your membership in a particular culture.

This revised conception of edification, and the concerns about the partiality of pragmatist reason that motivated the revision, suggest that Rorty's liberalism is seriously flawed because it addresses the wrong problem. It was formulated to resolve the conflict between edifying individual and conversational culture, but our discussion has disclosed a prior source of conflict: that between a culture favored by one language of pragmatist reasons and a culture handicapped by that language. This conflict shapes our self-formation, in that reasons that reinforce our identification with one culture will also serve as reasons to distinguish ourselves invidiously from another. When we acknowledge that pragmatist reasoning is bound to provoke cultural antagonism, then, we can see that Rorty's liberalism cannot do the job of reducing social conflict. Nor is it needed any longer to reconcile conversation and edification, for both of these processes now work together to form members of cultures in a context of necessary social conflict. Like the old problem of consciousness, liberalism becomes a fifth wheel.

This link between cultural antagonism and self-formation has been powerfully articulated by the deconstructionist political theorists Ernesto Laclau and Chantal Mouffe, in *Hegemony and Socialist Strategy*.[22] They argue that, rather than conceiving of antagonism as a fall from grace from some Arcadian social state to which we can and should return, antagonism is part of the original, constitutive impulse to form and maintain a culture. It motivates each of us to invest in contingently available discourses of interests and values which grant an identity by distinguishing *us* from *them*. Laclau and Mouffe make a compelling case that democracies suffer more when they try to delegitimize and suppress such antagonism altogether, than when they acknowledge its constructiveness, and allow it to open up as many alternative cultures as possible.

Proceeding from this perspective, Laclau, in the essay "Community and Its Paradoxes: Richard Rorty's 'Liberal Utopia'," examines Rorty's separation of the public and private realms.[23] His critical reservations cogently summarize my own as well:

> Is the realm of personal self-realization really a *private* realm? It would be so if that self-realization took place in a neutral medium in which individuals could seek unimpeded the fulfillment of their own aims. But this medium is, of course, a myth. A woman searching for her self-realization will find obstacles in the form of male-oriented rules that will limit her personal aspirations and possibilities. The feminist struggles tending to change those rules will constitute a collective "we" different from the "we" of the abstract public citizenship, but the space that these struggles create—remember the motto "the personal is the political"—will be no less a communitarian and public space than the one in which political parties intervene and in which elections are fought. And the same can be said, of course, of any struggle that begins as a result of the existence of social norms, prejudices, regulations, and so forth that frustrate the self-realization of an individual. . . . So, what about the private? It is a residual category, limited to those aspects of our activity in which our objectives are not interfered with by any structural social barrier, in which their achievement does not require the constitution of any struggling community, of any "we."[24]

For the distinction between the public and private realms, Laclau substitutes distinctions between different public realms, different cultures. He redefines the private realm as being socially unproblematic, and so of little political interest; the "public realm," in contrast, is by definition problematic, and so perpetually giving birth to plural, antagonistic realms. He then seconds "the personal is the political" to stress that edification is an activity which puts at stake more than just an individual's selfhood. By redescribing herself or himself, and so mutating a culture's language, the person edifying herself or himself intervenes in a public space which broaches new possibilities and threats for many others, and thus gathers together new political identities. This process continually challenges democratic societies to respond with ingenious expansions and compromises in order to keep open as many horizons of edification as possible. As a condition for this flourishing political life, therefore, such a democracy should acknowledge that the question, *Whose values?* may be pertinently asked of any discourse that would take for granted the stable constitution of a "we" or an "I"—and thus a "them." This question reminds us that we may always respond to our identification in some established, commonsensical discourse as a "them" by declaring our independence from it for the sake of edification; this is a defining characteristic of democratic life. Yet unlike Emerson, who would see in such a democratic declaration of independence an affirmation of self-reliance, Laclau affirms by this declaration the always-open possibility of relying on a different band of others, of becoming a member of a different culture.

> So, as we see, the classical terms of the problem are displaced: it is no longer a question of preventing a public space from encroaching upon that of private individuals, given that the public spaces have to be constituted in order to achieve individual aims. But the condition for a democratic society is that these public spaces have to be plural: a democratic society is, of course, incompatible with the existence of only *one* public space. [25]

Still, the public realms that such conversational edification multiplies are antagonistic to each other; antagonism is both the spur to, and the result of, edification. Laclau and Mouffe invite us less to eliminate conflict between the aims of edification and conversation, as to reposition that conflict on the boundaries between cultures, where it may be dealt with more openly by all of those who have a stake in it, where it may be dealt with more "democratically." Much of this antagonism is expressed in the question: *Whose values?* Responding to this question, members of a given culture may assert their freedom to redescribe themselves in contrast to their culture's values, and to constitute a new culture that holds antagonistic values. In other words, they may simultaneously answer, *Not* my values! and, Not *my* values! *Your values!*

The violence of that closing epithet troubles me. Unlike Laclau and Mouffe, I am not prepared to accept its necessity. Who could do that for its fatal victims? Granted we should not pretend it is not there, or simply overpower it with righteousness; nevertheless, can we not experiment with ways of forming new cultures which entail less destructive costs? This hope is, of course, full of perilous traps, particularly the one that Foucault has repeatedly pointed out, of falling for a utopian project demanding yet another machinery of power, but I do not see any reason why it should be inherently unrespectable. [26] In particular, I wonder if it is not possible to ask questions like, *Whose values?* in a distinctly different tone, so that they might broach a cultural conversation that is disarming.

My concluding chapter will attempt to do just that. This chapter has distanced Rorty's conception of conversational edification from any metaphysical interpretation, and has tied it instead to liberal education in the service of experimental, democratic, cultural reform. We have run into a problem, however, with the liberalist, public-private distinction on which Rorty relies to cope with conflict between the edifying individual and her or his conversational culture. The distinction cannot resolve the conflict because it cannot be neutrally established; it can only be drawn in a situation in a way that favors one group of people over another. Moreover, this partiality infects pragmatist reasoning in general, and necessarily sets cultures of conversational edification against each other. Can we reduce this tendency to cultural conflict? Can we do this in liberal education? If we cannot, then will we not be trapped in a nihilistic society?

I believe that we can if we emphasize the role of aporetic questioning in such education. While maintaining a distance from the claims of metaphysics, perhaps a better understanding of this role will help us appreciate the need to reconnect this new philosophy of liberal education to a more traditional experience of the longing that inspired, and can still inspire, metaphysical questions. Such a longing is not only one for the heroic life, but also one for a life in a morally perfectionist culture, coexisting peacefully with others.

6

DISARMING CULTURE
THROUGH THE PERFECTIONIST
LOVE OF LIBERAL LEARNING

The past four chapters have discussed how Rorty's work strengthens Dewey's case against Hutchins's conception of liberal education. They have left us facing two challenges. On the one hand, we now have further reason to distrust Hutchins's conception of a metaphysical liberal education grounded on epistemology; such an epistemology is prone to promote authoritarian forms of intellectual and social order insofar as it originates in a resentful reaction to the creative will to power of others. On the other hand, Rorty's conception of conversational edification in the service of liberalism, which develops Dewey's pragmatist conception of liberal education, appears prone to perpetuate antagonism between fragmenting cultures. Both challenges thus threaten the capacity of liberal education to foster a democratic social life.

Since I have been building on—and have been edified by—Rorty's work, I am inclined to put these challenges in the form of the following, hopefully constructive question: Can his conception of conversational edification be revised to make it not only antimetaphysical but also antiantagonistic, that is, culturally pacifistic? Can we reconceive of conversational edification as a process that indeed forms cultures, however not by setting off one discourse of values against another, but by disarming those who join the conversation, and by inviting interlocutors to commit themselves, their sense of self, to this disarming culture?

I believe that we can, if we detach conversational edification from its Rortyan and Deweyan affirmation of pragmatist values, and attach it instead to a nonmetaphysical affirmation of moral perfectionism. Conversational edification would, accordingly, be a process which initiates you neither into a metaphysical nor a pragmatist culture, but into an affiliation with others oriented to the aporetic question of perfection. By explaining how this initiation may take place, I hope to conclude this study by showing how a perfectionist love of liberal learning could help us reenvision the scene of liberal education in a multiculturally pacifistic context.

To examine the nature and value of this perfectionist love of learning, I would like to step back from the book's argument so far, and to turn to a relatively naive question on the border between education and philosophy. My hope is that, by proceeding from this question, I will be able to develop Rorty's idea of conversational edification in a way that both clarifies its value for educators, and responds to the problem of cultural antagonism.

If you were an educator, say a teacher or a principal, why might you be interested in philosophy? One possible reason is that you are a philosophy teacher, or administrator of a philosophy program, another is that you are responsible for organizing a field of course offerings, and so need to know whether and how philosophy should be a part of it. Finally, philosophy may not play a role in your educational work but may address other, nonprofessional dimensions of your life.

All of these reasons make sense. But I would like to press the question toward still other possibilities. Suppose that you were in none of the positions mentioned above. Say you are a biology teacher uninterested in philosophy. Could there be any other reasons, rooted in your educational vocation, for you to get interested?

Two more possibilities come to mind. A first reason is that doubt about the value of your educational efforts may draw you to speculate on their ultimate philosophical purpose. You might wonder about whether the world, or at least the part of it with which you are involved, has a fundamental order, and whether there is a way to conduct teaching and learning about biology such that these activities, and the other activities they affect, are properly and happily in harmony with that order. The answers to these questions would give you confidence that there is something meaningfully good about such learning and teaching, something that redeems their hardships and failures. It would then make sense that a promising way to discover these answers is through philosophical study, since, more than any other discipline, philosophy reputedly addresses the deepest questions of life in a systematic way, with a minimum of unexamined assumptions. Hence your desire to know the ultimate purpose of your educational work may lead you to take an interest in philosophy.

A second possible reason is that problems your work runs into may draw you to try out potentially useful, philosophically disciplined methods of thinking. Perhaps you are struggling with certain ethical dilemmas, or perhaps you are trying to get a clearer grasp of the advantages and disadvantages of different pedagogical approaches. Since philosophy names not only a body of propositional knowledge that such-and-such is true, but also a body of practical know-how exemplified in proven techniques of analysis, argumentation, and theory construction, you may find in it tools with which to attack such problems. So even if you are not especially concerned about ideas of ultimate purpose, you may be interested in mastering and employing philosophical reasoning for more immediate educational purposes.

These two reasons for educators to become interested in philosophy have, in one way or another, inspired most of the work in American philosophy of education, as Jonas F. Soltis observed in his state-of-the-field overview in the early eighties. [1] But let us suppose that an antipathy to the philosophy you studied in college—an antipathy hardened by the last philosopher you studied, Richard Rorty—prevents you from being impressed by these reasons. As you learned about one grand, metaphysical worldview after another, the notion that anyone could capture the profound complexities of life in a unitary system of essential ideas appeared increasingly delusive and pretentious. Better to go through life with a cautious grip on the partiality and provisionality of your own individual and cultural beliefs, you were convinced. At the same time, what was being

touted in other philosophy classes as invaluable or inevitable method-
ologies of inquiry and argument struck you as too removed from
the rush of life outside the armchair. Your biological work was
instilling in you more than enough "critical thinking" skills, ones
which seemed more sensitive to the experience of actual practice.
Foolishly or not, then, you are interested neither in systems of
thought determining educational purpose, nor in techniques of reasoning for educational problem-solving. Is there any other way to
interest you in philosophy?

Let me give you a "problem" student. Your nickname for him
is "Alceste" because his character so resembles that of the title figure
in Molière's *The Misanthrope*. Alceste just wants to be left alone.
Everywhere he looks, he is always complaining, he sees pretentious-
ness, hypocrisy, and phoniness protected by complacent callousness.
He knows, he is forever claiming, that what is truly demanded of
us is to speak, to declare ourselves, with sincere feeling. But he has
learned that such speech makes him either a laughingstock and
dupe in his community, or a threat to be isolated. So rather than
compromise, he has chosen isolation. Or as Molière's Alceste puts
it in his final, departing lines:

> Meanwhile, betrayed and wronged in everything,
> I'll flee this bitter world where vice is king,
> And seek some spot unpeopled and apart
> Where I'll be free to have an honest heart. [2]

In your class, Alceste's mood and conduct swing from rude righteousness to stony withdrawal to surprising naïveté. A third of the time
you are furious with his temerity, a third you are exasperated with
his indifference, and a third smiling at his childlikeness. Yet whatever
state he is in, he does not want to learn anymore. He refuses to
listen, he says again and again, because he does not respect either
the worth of what you are teaching or your worthiness to teach. As
you talk to him, he seems to lie in wait for incidental inconsistencies
to pop up, which he then blows up into melodramas about the
meaning of life. He accuses the enterprise of education in particular,
and of knowing in general, of trying to cover up the arbitrariness

of all things, and so the absurdity of any particular state of affairs. He alone refuses to flee the truly humbling questions. Impossible. Thus you and he seem to speak two completely different languages. How can you reach him, let alone encourage him to learn?

Here is a particular educational challenge, one which I trust rings true to some of our memories of youth, one which may plague more than one teacher. It is a challenge to your pedagogical efforts coming from someone on the threshold of becoming an active, self-conscious participant in a culture. In Rorty's and Laclau's terms, this person is starting to identify himself as a member of a conversational culture and an ironic antagonist of other cultures; he is becoming acculturated in the expectations, aspirations, and struggles of a particular community. His development in this direction is blocked, however, by a wave of disgust with those expectations, expectations which he associates less with the particular culture than with adulthood in general. Unless you can figure out how to reinterest Alceste in active membership in this culture, or in some other culture, he seems destined to drop out into a culturally unreflective world of childhood.

What can help you do that, I propose, is philosophy. How so? And if so, why would this proposal be any different from one to offer philosophy as a pragmatic tool for solving educational problems? Would it not be merely narrower, in that it targets only one problem? Moreover, if this problem is youth's suspicion that life is meaningless, then obviously a constructive response would be for the teacher to propound a truer, more comprehensive worldview full of meaning. How would an interest in that response differ from the other interest in philosophy as a metaphysical system of ideas illuminating the order of things? Even if I can explain how philosophy could help an educator help a misanthrope to learn, therefore, this reason for educators to be interested in it may not significantly differ from either of the previous two reasons, reasons representing the Hutchinsian and Deweyan legacies we are trying to distance ourselves from.

Before I develop this proposal and reply to these reservations, let me stress the suggestion in it that educators may become interested in philosophy in response to a problem that is less philosophical than educational. Something seems to be preventing Alceste from learning. Such a problem may be, and has been, approached using other disciplines (for instance, politics, psychology, religion, and so forth). Philosophers tackling it must take up the burden of establishing what makes a philosophical approach both different from others, and especially helpful. The value of this approach would then be clear, even to those who have no use or taste for its technical language. Only in this way may philosophy draw the sincere interest of such challenged educators.

What would an educationally constructive response to Alceste, distinctly informed by philosophy that is neither metaphysical nor pragmatist, look like? An example I would like to explore is offered by Stanley Cavell in "A Cover Letter to Molière's *Misanthrope.*" It opens, "DEAR ALCESTE."[3] Cavell proceeds to share with Alceste musings about what he calls the "discovery of adolescence," and about how this discovery is reflected in works as various as Thoreau's *Walden*, Shakespeare's *Othello*, and Montaigne's *Essays*, among others. These musings all serve an explicit purpose.

> You see that I would try to tempt you back, to tell you that there are those in the world who have not forgotten what you know, hence who feel the rebuke in your taking offense. But it is up to you and to us in our separate ways; it is pointless to beg, and this is not the time to harangue.[4]

Why does Cavell respond to Molière's drama by directly addressing one of its fictional characters? Why does he *tell* Alceste that he is trying to *tempt* him back to society? How is this temptation related to the realization that others may feel rebuked by Alceste? And how do Cavell's words, acknowledging his and Alceste's separate ways, differ from begging or haranguing or, for that matter, from an educator's, a philosophy professor's, lecturing? These questions start to get at what makes his response philosophical, encouraging of learning, and morally perfectionist.

What differentiates the response from a harangue or lecture starts
to emerge after an opening which does hold forth rather laboriously:

> I will not disguise from you my conviction that your position is
> intellectually indefensible. What more really can you say on your
> behalf but that human society is filled with show, with artifice, with
> insincerity, with dissociations between the public and the private,
> between the outer and the inner? And what more really need be said
> in reply to you than to concede this, and whatever follows from it,
> as the very essence of the civilized; and then simply request that
> you—what? Let us not say either love civilization or leave it. The
> request is rather that you not be illogical: if you do decide to join
> the human race; or let me say, to take your place in society; then
> do not complain that you will not by that act have rejoined the world
> of nature. It need not be denied that in this decision something is
> lost. But need you deny that something is gained, something indeed
> human? To see these two sides is just to grow up, something you
> are heartily advised to do.[5]

Hear, hear! everyone but Alceste might exclaim. Cavell is sensibly
pointing out that human existence just *is* given to artifice, but that
to accept this is to gain an essential part of your humanity. Although
this acceptance may cost Alceste part of his integrity, if he lets go
of his one-sidedness (integrity clung to fanatically), he will be able
to understand and appreciate the deep significance of that loss,
how it threads through, ties together, and qualifies any assertive
righteousness. He may discover, then, that his loss is shared by,
and puts him in touch with, many other human beings.

So is this what philosophy has to offer you or any other teacher
in this predicament: a case for why Alceste should adopt a more
balanced view of society's hypocrisy, one which is both metaphysically informed and logically sound? Not quite. For as Cavell immediately goes on to observe, such an argument, authoritatively delivered,
is not the end of the matter:

> The issue is not so much why you are not convinced by the better
> arguments of the others. That sort of impasse is hardly news in hu-
> man affairs. The issue is rather why the others care that you are not
> convinced. You are without power. What is your hold upon them?
> What do you represent to them?[6]

Cavell imagines that Alceste, like many, may not be convinced by metaphysical or logical reasons he is nevertheless unable to answer: such people are often called unreasonable. They, in turn, may likewise dismiss those arguments, punctuated with such name-calling, as so much harangue. But Cavell is intrigued that, even if the dialogue threatens to reach such an impasse because Alceste turns a deaf ear to reason, he and others may be unwilling to turn a deaf ear to Alceste. Something about Alceste and what he stands for awakens concern and devotion, and a commitment to find, if need be, another way to reach him. Beyond Alceste's unreasonableness, Cavell finds himself listening to something about Alceste's tone.

Why? Cavell traces the tone's "powerless power" to Alceste's "purity." In response to the last question in the quoted passage above, he speculates that "you represent purity to their purity, or to their sense of their purity lost—not as if corrupted exactly, but as if misplaced, thus still present somehow."[7] He does not define purity beyond equating it with "innocence." I understand him to mean by both terms a sense of what is good, in general and in a particular situation, uncompromised by practical or systematic considerations and judgments; thus an intuition or sentiment of goodness that lifts us by surprise prior to any determined search for it. Accordingly, the path to mature insight into the good leads us back to, and keep us appreciatively in touch with, childhood spontaneity and the sheer joy of being alive. This interpretation suggests that when this pure joy—what Rousseau called *"le sentiment de l'existence"*—is critically objectified and articulated as a system of ideals, it may, like innocence, be lost, with only its absence dialectically indicating that it must be somewhere to be remembered.[8] In the meantime, I might instead place my sense of goodness in a set of observations, beliefs, actions, or habits that do not actually feel good, that feel forced. Thus what Alceste represents, in his aversion to placing his purity in society, is someone who reminds me of what I may have misplaced, someone who is still innocently independent from reasoning that, however logically binding and powerful, does not always move me to rejoice in being. In the face of the world's arguments, he declares: What I feel, what moves me to love life, I must have knowledge of. And in the face of that declaration, we may start to recognize that those arguments do not entirely speak for us, that what they partially drown out is also ours: Alceste's sincere heart.

What draws Cavell to Alceste is the appeal of sincerity, of being true to what moves you—but what draws Alceste away from such society is the smell of hypocrisy. To reach Alceste, this aversion needs to be understood, particularly in relation to the sincerity that calls for the reaching gesture. Cavell pairs the perception of the hypocrisy of society with an inward awareness of self-division or "fraudulence"; he explains how these moral perceptions together form the predicament of adolescent dissociation:

> The hypocrite would dissociate himself or herself from a life of human vulnerabilities, call it human nature; the antihypocrite would dissociate himself or herself from a world of invulnerable pretenses. If adolescence will level the most unforgiving charge of hypocrisy at those ahead of it, it will level against itself an equally unforgiving charge of fraudulence—and the one because of the other. The world posed before it, beckoning it, is a field of possibilities, toward which curiosity is bound to outreach commitment.[9]

Alceste and other adolescents charge the adult world with hypocrisy because it teaches them to protect themselves by blinding themselves, by overlooking vulnerabilities in others so that they may likewise be spared. But in attacking such a defensive pact of pretenses, Alceste evokes an alternative world of candor that he has yet to live in. The fraudulence that he must suspect of himself, if he is to be consistent in his suspicion of the hypocrisy of others, is that he may not be able either to renounce the indulgent support of the familial and familiar world. This plight, Cavell remarks, makes adolescence:

> . . . inherently a time of theater, of self-consciousness presented as embarrassment, of separation from the familiar, of separation from the self, as if something were tearing; of a scrutiny that claims to know everything directing itself upon feelings and actions that can claim to know nothing.[10]

Cavell's use of the phrase "human vulnerabilities" above is curious; I would have expected him to refer to human flaws or foibles with regard to hypocrisy. Perhaps, though, vulnerability better gets at what unites—in its dividing of the self—the hypocrite and the anti-hypocrite. I would gloss this vulnerability as that of dwelling in the shadow, the night, of unanswerable questions, those which threaten joy with a deeper unenlightenment and a more serious shame. The hypocrite pretends that the questions which could unsettle your happy and meaningful sense of yourself have been definitively answered; he or she tacitly agrees not to raise them about you if you do the same regarding him or her. The antihypocrite breaks this pact by attacking that pretense; however, his or her own unwillingness to submit that criticism, and the self-assurance that flows from it, in turn to such questions marks it with fraudulent evasion. In both cases, the questions call us to recognize that we do not ultimately and honestly know what we are doing or why, and so cannot comfortably take our feelings of joy for a mark of goodness. They render us both vulnerable to Rortyan humiliation. This recognition, combined with the recognition that we nevertheless persist in assuming that our actions and feelings have moral significance, keeps dissociated the questioning self from the self in question, the purposeful self from the absurd stranger within. We may also recognize in this dissociation the plight that calls for moral perfectionism, as Cavell understood it in the passage that opened this book:

> Moral Perfectionism's contribution to thinking about the moral necessity of making oneself intelligible (one's actions, one's suffering, one's position) is, I think it can be said, its emphasis before all on becoming intelligible to oneself, as if the threat to one's moral coherence comes most insistently from that quarter, from one's sense of obscurity to oneself, as if we are subject to demands we cannot formulate, leaving us unjustified, as if our lives condemn themselves.

Such an interpretation of the vulnerability, the self-unintelligibility, at the heart of this predicament jibes with another closed-minded reaction to it on the part of adult society.

> . . . Instead of opening secrets to you, it [adult society] informs you that it has none, that what you see is all there is to it. Hence to its recruits it is now reduced merely to *saying* "Grow up."[11]

Recall that Cavell's initial philosophical harangue said just this. In contrast, this passage suggests that Alceste's "childish" intuition, that there must be something more he must be, might actually be a guide to a company of questioners. Instead of trying to argue Alceste down, what if a culture, call it a philosophical culture, were to "open secrets" to him, showing him how unavoidable mysteries, figures of *sophia*, bring us together into an intelligible and heartfelt affiliation, a *philia*? I shall return to this suggestion.

The adolescent perception of hypocrisy and fraudulence, then, focuses on self-dissociation condemned in the adult and threatening the adolescent, a self-dissociation broached by our vulnerability to unanswerable questions. This self-dissociation in turn opens up a necessary moment of discontinuity between generations, a moment when a society and culture, rather than being automatically inherited, must be chosen by the newcomer. It is because the drama between Cavell and Alceste concerns this intracultural discontinuity that it is not one of intercultural antagonism. Alceste is not rejecting one culture in favor of another, as if he spies some other culture untainted by hypocrisy that he could just move to. Indeed, part of the reason he has to suspect himself of being a fraud is that he doubts there could be such a culture, there could be a mode of human life that is purely antihypocritical. Any culture he enters, by virtue of its conversational and edifying qualities, will subject his purity to the influence of other members. As long as he remains confused and anxious about what such influence will mean for him, for his childhood affirmations, he will be resistant not in the name of a counterhegemonic cultural project, but of his precious, if uncommunicable, isolating memories.

Another way of differentiating this moment of intracultural discontinuity from that of intercultural antagonism is by the tone of the questions that accompany them. As we discussed in the previous chapter, the Nietzschean question, Whose values? moves you to adopt a polemical position vis-à-vis some set of values that is not your own. It proceeds from a recognition that the culture with which you are identifying is caught up in a struggle for not-unlimited resources, and so it spurs you to make yourself morally intelligible by invidiously distinguishing yourself from members of competing cultures, and by asserting the right of your culture to a measure of hegemony. In contrast, the questions to which the hypocrite and the antihypocrite, Cavell and Alceste, are together vulnerable are questions that lack that polemical tone. These questions threaten the capacity of Alceste to affiliate his childhood with any culture, and the capacity of Cavell's adult culture—the one to which I am imagining Alceste nominally to belong—to reproduce itself. They are prior to the question, Whose values? insofar as they seriously raise the possibility that nothing may be of value for Alceste or for a culture that cannot hold those like him; haunting this possibility is the despairing denouement of adolescent violence and suicide. What is nonetheless promising about these questions, though, is the other possibility that they could disarm our initiation into a culture before the polemical question, Whose values? gets off the ground. This promise, I shall explain later, stands to make them crucial for a multicultural, liberal education.

Being a newcomer to his culture, then, Alceste is challenged to consent to a prior, supposedly unquestionable order of things, one that distinguishes the achievement of adulthood. It is the withholding of this consent that alienates him as an adolescent, and turns his future into a drama of overcoming self-conscious isolation:

> . . . You represent the discovery of adolescence, of that moment at which the worth of adulthood is—except, I suppose, to deep old age—most clearly exposed; at which adulthood *is* the thing you are asked to choose, to consent to. Naturally your choice will be based on insufficient evidence. But woe to them that believe the choice is easy, that in forgoing adolescence you forgo little of significance. They have merely forgotten what they have lost. . . .[12]

Alceste appears to have the following choice. Either he may consent to join the world of hypocritical adulthood, and so throw away his purity. Or he may reject that world misanthropically, and so confine his purity to a "beforeworld" of childhood. Or he may deny that there is a significant or difficult choice to be made at all, because "people" just automatically and inevitably grow up—a denial typical of those who are already grown up—and so lose even the chance to consent. In this choice, what is at stake is the value that adult membership in a culture may have for Alceste, whether it will cost him his purity, and whether that cost is too high. Also at issue is whether the self-conscious deliberation that is a condition for choosing will stifle any actual choice. To return once more to Cavell's words that opened this book: Can Alceste find a sociable language that would render him intelligible to himself and to others, a language that carries "perfectionism's emphasis on culture or cultivation?" Can he find "direction in what seems a scene of moral chaos, the scene of a dark place in which one has lost one's way?"

Suppose Alceste could have faith that, however much his purity may be tested by adult society, it will not be lost. Suppose he could confidently allow his innocent joys to be affected by others, taught by them, without thereby fearing that this affection would corrupt them, and cause him to misplace them in a learned affectation of someone else's experience. And suppose, in addition to such faith, he could find a reason to want to place his pure joy in society where it could be educated. Would he not then be able to affirm the value of adult society as precisely the value of having to choose adulthood, and so having to confront, doubtless repeatedly, what is risky about his future with others? A risk that gives joy passion, and turns it into a constant love?

Cavell locates the seeds of this faith and desire in Alceste's heart and what that heart cannot deny being attracted to:

> Purity can only know by its own heart and by the encouragement of what draws it. So if I maintain the right of experience to its arguments for consent, I equally maintain the right of innocence to give and to withhold its consent without argument, on the basis of its feeling, its sense of itself. The world needs that sense, requires that you say, willingly, that the world is good enough to want to live in. And I assume that in general you, in general youth, wish to want the world; which is to say: you wish to be presented with a world you can want, to which you can give yourself.[13]

Alceste longs for companionship and for a world in which he belongs. But whether he will give himself to this particular world, resolutely, and where he will place his innocence in it, depends on whether something or someone in it attracts his heart. Furthermore, whether he sincerely feels such an attraction is something that only he can discover and acknowledge; the feeling cannot be prescribed by arguments that he ought to be attracted to such-and-such, or that he is attracted but is unconscious that he is. (Of course I am not saying that ethical or psychoanalytic arguments have no place in this self-examination, only that after they say their piece, they have to silently leave room for examination.) Therefore to join society, Alceste requires the freedom to love. And if he does consent to join, and is not simply forced to submit, then part of what may have attracted him to this company is precisely that it respects this freedom because it celebrates sincere feeling as a sign of life and responsive friendship. Such a society celebrates desire for membership as a sign of cultural vitality.

It is this yearning of Alceste's to be attracted to something or someone that Cavell's attraction to Alceste meets. Alceste wants sincerity, but all he sees is hypocrisy and, in himself, immorally unintelligible fraudulence; hence he withdraws in despair from an undesirable world. Cavell, however, sees and is morally drawn to Alceste's sincerity, despite the latter's misanthropic unreasonableness. For these two to affirm a common world, a friendship, then, Alceste would have to discover his own, hidden sincerity in Cavell, and Cavell his own, less hypocritical, more moral reason in Alceste. Cavell would have to acknowledge what Alceste's sincerity, his expressive joy, has reasonably to teach him, assuming he sincerely cares about helping Alceste to find moral intelligibility. To return again to this book's opening quotation, Cavell would have to acknowledge the responsibilities of the friend, "the figure, let us say, whose conviction in one's moral intelligibility draws one to discover it, to find words and deeds in which to express it, in which to enter the conversation of justice."

He starts to do this by asking for Alceste's consent to their company rather than claiming it, say, on the authority vested in him by logic or common sense or the law. He introduces this request by telling Alceste that "there are those in the world who have not forgotten what you know, hence who feel the rebuke in your taking offence."

I read this now as his confession that Alceste's innocent tone has reminded him that there is something dangerously divided about his own heart. In response, then, he warns about his desire to "tempt" Alceste back, as if he wants Alceste to check his possibly hypocritical words against the standard of that tone, as if he wants to encourage Alceste to believe in what is sincerely felt and loved above all. He allows that, after hearing him out, Alceste may find that his request is insincere, and so may continue on a separatist path. With his guard thus down, he will then have to absorb a painful lesson about himself and what he has "misplaced." It is because Cavell does allow this, and does put his own self-understanding at stake, that he keeps his request from turning into counterproductive, and so pointless, begging.

And why would Alceste not reject the request? Even if he is looking for a world to which he can belong, would not Cavell's confession of self-dissociation repel him? Indeed, was this not precisely why he abandoned his beloved in Molière's play, Célimène, when she confessed her hypocrisy?

What discloses Cavell's suitability as a conversation partner for Alceste, and the suitability of the other authors with whom Cavell is in conversation, is Cavell's express capacity to see what Alceste sees. Unlike Célimène, who declares that she is ready to attach herself to Alceste, but in the same breath adds that she cannot detach herself from the society at odds with Alceste—a declaration that, however reasonable, Alceste takes to be more double-talk—Cavell makes no such declaration. He appears to bank instead on Alceste discovering on his own that they are *semblables*, together at a loss as to how to live. For this reason, his response does not so much propose solutions to the predicament of adolescence, as it develops a more insightful and sensitive sympathy to that predicament. His response demonstrates that it is possible for adolescence to grow into questioning, philosophical adulthood without betraying the purity that cast doubt on the given world of answers.

Cavell views the predicament of adolescence less as a problem to be solved with philosophical knowledge or know-how, with the two interests in philosophy described earlier, and more as an opportunity for youths to be initiated into, and adults to recollect, the mysteries that keep us honest and together. This view is expressed by his tendency to raise questions to which he ventures no answers. Consider, for example, the following meditation on his father's grace:

> But I remember instances of my father in conversation with strangers—in a shop, a lobby, a train—animated, laughing, comparing notes, when the charge of insincerity fell from my grasp and I would gaze at his behavior as at a mystery. How can he care enough what the other thinks to be provident of his good feeling, and yet not care so terribly as to become unable to provide it? What skill enables him to be the one that puts the other at ease? Where can he have acquired it? He knew no more about the other than the other knew about him. He seemed merely able to act on what nobody could fail to know, and to provide what nobody could fail to appreciate, even if in a given moment they could not return it. Call it sociability.[14]

The last term is not an answer to these questions, let alone their hortative moral, but a name for their field in which Cavell's confidence, at least, is suspended. In admitting that his experiences, assumptions, and ideas trail off into such an awful and awesome, sublime aporia, he exposes himself to the sight of what Alceste sees: that the point of living is at every instant and forever beyond our grasp. So to communicate this view of things, he employs questions as tropes that communicate, with what he says in "foregrounding" words, the necessary background of the mysteriously unsayable, the hidden reason, the *cosmos absconditus*. Such questions show Alceste how it may be possible to participate in an alternative discourse that stays true to what adolescence doubts about the given discourse. They show Alceste that he is not alone in what he sees or feels.

At the same time, however, these are questions *to* Alceste, calling for a response if not an answer. They thus repeatedly stress Cavell's opening gesture of writing about adolescence in the form of a letter, a form which personally addresses someone, often in reply to being so addressed. As tropes, then, they express not only sublimity but intimacy. They communicate an interest in Alceste's reply, and a confidence that the reply will further Alceste's and Cavell's conversation and bond. The aporetic nature of the questions should encourage Alceste and Cavell to affirm that, despite all differences, they share the same sense of honesty, neither of them pretending to know hypocritically or fraudulently what they do not. And this common ignorance ought to mean that they have something to say to each other about how to respond to it, live with it.

But if nothing can answer these questions, then are not Alceste and Cavell condemned to a society that can only be nihilistic? I do not believe so, because something *does* respond to the questions, even in the absence of answers. This something is life or being itself, its groundless, spontaneous, and gratuitous revelation. That is the miracle—and recognized as such, as a response out of nowhere to our acknowledgment of the questionableness of our lives, the revelation of miraculous being can be a sign of perfection that gives moral direction, pointing for each of us the way out of the "dark place" in which we got lost. Here we do not orient ourselves to perfection by understanding it metaphysically as a necessary ideal. Rather, we affirm perfection as contingent grace; it is contingent because its revelation takes place without any necessary, only questionable, cause or reason, and it is grace because its revelation awakens in us the *sentiment de l'existence* that blessed our childhood, and that can keep our adult actions meaningfully fulfilling. I realize that my remarks here border on the ineffable, but perhaps those who find some sense in them (and who understand why inarticulacy at this point is inevitable) will see why I agree with Cavell in calling this response to the drama of adolescence "perfectionist."

Cavell, then, is calling Alceste to recognize their kinship. Alceste may then discover that there is a way for him to stay himself in the world, a way which may attract him back into a communion with respected equals such that he once more wants to learn from them about himself, and consents to such learning. If Cavell's response does prove capable of transforming Alceste's lonely longing into sociable consent, then it will have also demonstrated the value of so placing purity where purity can gain a voice, and reach disheartened youth. It may even inspire Alceste to join those who have dedicated themselves to keeping that voice alive.

Since Alceste's recognition of Cavell has to overcome suspicions about whether purity can survive adult society, it cannot be based on shared beliefs alone, but must be based as well on Cavell's demonstrated capacity to move Alceste with his own surviving purity, his own lyrically troped tone. This tone is expressed not in reasoned answers that Cavell advances, but in disturbing questions that he admits and readdresses to Alceste, questions that remind us of the value of childhood's joy, and that can revitalize that joy by evoking what morally threatens it. His response, then, suggests that philosophy may embrace that joyful purity as its calling. It suggests that philosophers may start to understand and distinguish their work by its aspiration to broach a questioning conversation with the misanthropes in us all.

Indeed, a last feature to notice about the response is that it draws the philosopher Cavell to still others who share his predicament.

> . . . The side of me that sides with you has in recent years repeatedly found itself siding with those for whom the relation between innocence and experience is their life, call it the relation between their past of possibilities and the present actuality of the world, or between their memories of being disappointed and their fears of being disappointing.[15]

Does this passage not capture the high drama in the educator's conscience? Could it be that educators may be able to recognize themselves as well in this philosophical passion?

Proceeding from Cavell's example, then, what would a philosopher have to offer that is of interest to you, a biology teacher? And how would this differ from what thinkers in other disciplines have to offer?

I have suggested that philosophy can be considered, among other things, a discipline and tradition of keeping purity alive in the midst of social compromise, so that a culture may continue to attract youth and thereby further its adventure. Accordingly, philosophy takes the very questions which drive adolescents away from a society of hypocritical answers, and tropes them so that these questions instead initiate adolescents into the moral vulnerability and innocent joy they share with their culture, and remind adults of their faith in that shared life. In this fashion, it recovers the central role that questioning, rather than argument, had in the Socratic response to the sophists; it reaffirms a treasure of its childhood. Philosophy is thus the name of a discourse in which the sincerely unsure (a complimentary closing for Cavell's letter?) find each other. It is the kind of discourse that promises to help you talk with, and not just to, the misanthropic student. To distinguish this understanding of philosophy from others, I shall call it, following Cavell, moral perfectionism.

Philosophers who expose you to this discourse, then, are offering you something different from what other disciplines offer. Indeed, they are offering something different from traditional philosophy of education. Their discourse does not claim to contain knowledge, let alone logical and metaphysical, foundational knowledge, of how to cause the misanthrope to learn. It scrupulously acknowledges that, prior to learning from you, youth must freely consent to associate with you. So to welcome this consent, it expresses how you, who have consented, still are moved by purity in a world of mystery, still possess a vital heart as well as head. Returning one last time to this book's opening quotation, morally perfectionist discourse expresses an educational concern (Cavell says "obsession") focused on "finding one's way rather than on getting oneself or another to take the way." Participants in this discourse thus hold open the door to a culture formed by the love of liberal learning.

Moreover, joining this culture transforms the identities of its members. To understand your encounter with Alceste in the morally perfectionist way we have been exploring means that you should no longer consider him to be merely a "misanthropic problem student." Rather, he is a purist who challenges you to reflect on your own purity at risk, and to revive and develop that purity, that capacity for sincere elevation, in a questioning conversation. He recalls you to the endless, characteristically adult adventure of liberal learning. Conversely, to consider Alceste in this way a teacher means that you should no longer consider yourself to be merely a "biology teacher." You are a liberal learner engaged with another liberal learner, together invigorating a culture of morally perfectionist questioning. Your efforts to teach biology touch sincerity when they are infused with a concern for your fellow learner's purity and a respect for their free consent. In your conversation with Alceste, then, the ways each of you understand yourselves, and the ways you relate to each other, develop. This development is a form of conversational edification.

This version of conversational edification differs from Rorty's principally in two respects. First, my morally perfectionist, conversational edification stresses the edifying power not of irony, but of aporetic questioning. This questioning is metaphysical insofar as it evokes the perfect reason for why things are the way they are, a reason that would, if articulable, conclusively reconcile the misanthrope to society. But because the questioning is aporetic, it does not lead to metaphysics. It keeps open the question of such a metaphysical reason out of an honest acknowledgment of human finitude—one which may incorporate some of Rorty's arguments—and a moral aversion to hypocrisy. It affirms, therefore, a less conclusive, more human reason to be reconciled to society: namely, that we are together vulnerable to what is sincerely unsure about our lives, but also are together graced by moments of joy. Questions expressing this vulnerability and grace can neither be dispelled of their sublime hold on us—though they can be repressed, hypocritically and fraudulently, even ironically, and so recollected educatively—nor definitively answered. For youth and adulthood to wonder, Why am I and this world here, what is our perfect reason for being? is to recognize together that to be a human self is to be in question.

This stress on aporetic questioning is linked to a second difference between Rorty's idea of conversational edification and mine: namely, their effects on culture. Rorty views the aim of conversational edification to be the formation of liberal ironists. In the last chapter, I argued that such an edification could succeed only at the price of also forming antagonistic cultures. The kind of conversational edification I am developing here, on the contrary, moderates cultural antagonism by qualifying any culture's claim to confident and authoritative knowledge or value. It develops the solidarity of youth and adulthood by drawing both to revere and learn from cultural works that keep alive sincere questioning. Such a culture of questions is, thus, in no position to assert its superior value over others, for it values the common vulnerability of its members, and so its capacity to disarm them and itself.

Indeed, members of this culture of questions are bound to be interested in what the cultural stranger can teach them. From such a stranger, they can learn how to recognize and respect alternative values and habits that raise new questions about their own, questions that reach into the hearts of their youth. For this reason, a culture of aporetic questioning will want to promote liberal learning that is multicultural. It will want to foster the likelihood that each member will have to face the cultural stranger, whose alternative terms of self-understanding expose the self-understanding of both to question-ableness. In such a scene of liberal learning, each may learn that we are all strangers to ourselves, together cast into an unfamiliar, *unheimlich* home. Behind diversity, a common sense of strangeness. Thus this process of conversational edification would not only foster a culture that is averse to conceiving of itself as superior to others, but would foster one that is positively interested in how other cultural understandings, respected in their integrity, can help keep its questions alive and its traditions regenerating.

If we understand liberal learning in terms of this conception of conversational edification, we may be able to affirm and develop the multicultural dimension of such learning without bogging ourselves down in a war against "the canon." Rather than review this all-too-familiar controversy, let me sketch out how I usually encounter it in my teaching. A lot of what I do consists of inviting prospective or actual teachers to converse with philosophical texts, in the hope that they might find such conversation edifying. Among other things, I try to encourage these students to recognize their better, more ideal selves, hopefully their teaching selves, in the ideas of these authors, and so to appreciate how the call to stand for something—for the good of teaching, for example—is continuous with the call to learn how to read the idealism of others. In this effort, I hope I am reflecting what I have learned from Rorty, Cavell, Oakeshott, and others. But of course, the effort is bound to meet its challenges.

One which I have encountered repeatedly is that some students refuse to recognize themselves in another's ideas, because they suspect that those ideas are rooted in a culture antagonistic to themselves and their ideals. Among students resistant to my invitation to find edification in European philosophy are those who belong to cultures that Europe has oppressively colonized. Since I come from such a culture myself, this challenge to philosophical learning has given me particular pause. Should I or anyone encourage students to recognize their ideal selves in the terms of an historically hostile culture? Would that be morally responsible teaching, given the ongoing struggle of members of dominated cultures to claim a voice of their own?

It would seem not, since the terms of such a hegemonic culture, especially when they claim to speak for universal human nature, are likely at least to obstruct the development of such a voice, and at worst to denigrate explicitly or implicitly these students' cultures. To encourage the students to recognize themselves in these terms, therefore, would be to invite them to accept a stultifying sense of selfhood. In my preface, I noted that this is a problem with Allan Bloom's "Great Books" approach to liberal education. It would seem, then, that I ought, rather, to encourage students in their mistrust of European culture and philosophy.

But this stance towards a "canon" of philosophical texts, a stance often associated with multiculturalist education conceived as a political movement of counterhegemonic resistance, also has its problem. On the one hand, the whole point of this resistance is to support the edifying projects of students who come from historically oppressed cultures, and to protect these projects from being unduly constrained. On the other hand, this political sensibility makes it easier for me, for example, to react to anything that questions my current self-understanding as a disrespectful attack. As long as cultural borders thus require fortification, I am unlikely to be drawn out of the confines of my current self-understanding, because I will always have reason to be dubious that anyone who comes from a "radically other" world could ever completely respect the way I see myself or my familiars see me. In such a suspicious and defensive posture, I would certainly be disinclined to learn from the philosophical texts of strangers how to describe myself and my world differently and perhaps more inspiringly. Thus my possibilities for edifying myself would be constrained after all.

So how should a teacher in my shoes, a teacher in a multicultural scene of liberal learning, respond to the "misanthropic" distrust that students may have of a cultural "canon?" As I have explained above, she or he could treat such texts neither as oracles of human nature nor as cultural idols, but as spurs to a questioning that envelops both author and reader. Such texts would then have nothing canonical or hegemonically threatening about them, for what we would ultimately respect in them are not their possessive claims to truth but the questions they broach beyond themselves, the intertextual, un-centered field of questions they lead us into. Of course they are most apt to provoke such questioning in students when they have the enduring power to keep such questioning alive in the teacher, when, that is, the teacher is still being sincerely edified by them. Thus I believe that considerations of teacher involvement, more than considerations of "cultural importance," should principally determine which texts are selected to be read in a course of liberal learning. The "canon" of the course should be deeply rooted in the edifying quest of the teacher, in the hope that it might help students to deepen their own quests.

In order to foster a culture that avoids the problems of metaphysical authoritarianism and cultural antagonism, then, I propose that we develop Rorty's idea of conversational edification in the following direction. We should sustain his antiauthoritarian critique of the epistemological foundations of metaphysics, and pursue his suggestion to replace epistemology with conversational edification as a way of understanding how cultures reform themselves. We should question, however, his liberalism's capacity to contain the ironic effects of edification in a private realm, and should recognize how such irony is bound to affect our public society as well. Recognizing this raises the problem of cultural antagonism, a problem that needs to be addressed if pragmatist reason is to be genuinely pragmatic. I recommend that we transform edification from a self-formative process that is ironic and private, to one that is aporetically questioning and culturally disarming. This conception of conversational edification would promote a culture that is morally perfectionist before it is pragmatist. Such a culture would build on the traditional hopes of democratic liberalism, but would protect them from the collapse of metaphysics and the spread of cynical opportunism by rooting them in an always-to-be renewed, free affirmation that young hearts have a home in the world. And the cultivation of this affirmation would help foster respect for and interest in other cultures.

To join this culture, you need only the courage to examine yourself honestly. As Cavell once observed, philosophical learning challenges us not because we need a special talent for it, a talent presumably conditioned by experience and background, but because we must dare to drop our protection against it and to expose ourselves to perennial discontent and longing.[16] Am I still in love with wisdom, with perfection? Thus the trouble with living continues—but in gratitude for what I am delivered over to?

NOTES

NOTES TO CHAPTER 1

1. Stanley Cavell, *Conditions Handsome and Unhandsome: The Constitution of Emersonian Perfectionism: The Carus Lectures, 1988* (Chicago: The University of Chicago Press, 1990), xxxi–xxxii.

2. John Dewey, *Democracy and Education: An Introduction to the Philosophy of Education* (New York: The Free Press, 1916), 332.

3. Michael Oakeshott, "A Place of Learning," in *The Voice of Liberal Learning: Michael Oakeshott on Education*, ed. Timothy Fuller (New Haven: Yale University Press, 1989), 41.

4. Plato, *The Collected Dialogues of Plato Including the Letters*, ed. Edith Hamilton and Huntington Cairns (Princeton: Princeton University Press, 1961), 18–19.

5. Michael Oakeshott, "The Study of Politics in a University," in *Rationalism in Politics and Other Essays*, with a Foreword by Timothy Fuller, new and exp. ed. (Indianapolis: Liberty Press, 1991), 189.

6. *Ibid.*, 192.

7. See René Descartes, *Discourse on Method and Meditations on First Philosophy*, trans. Donald A. Cress (Indianapolis: Hackett, 1980), 12–15.

8. Oakeshott, "The Study of Politics in a University," 187.

9. Stanley Cavell, "Who Disappoints Whom?" *Critical Inquiry*, no. 15 (Spring 1989): 606–607.

10. Allan Bloom, *The Closing of the American Mind: How Higher Education Has Failed Democracy and Impoverished the Souls of Today's Students*, with a Foreword by Saul Bellow (New York: Simon and Schuster Inc., 1987), 133.

11. See Cavell, *Conditions Handsome and Unhandsome*, 12–13.

12. Bloom, *The Closing of the American Mind*, 133.

13. *Ibid.*

14. The initial occasion for their exchange was the publication of Hutchins's book *The Higher Learning in America* (New Haven: Yale University

Press, 1936). Dewey reviewed the book in two articles: "Rationality in Education," *The Social Frontier*, 3, (December 1936): 71–73; and "President Hutchins' Proposals to Remake Higher Education," *The Social Frontier*, 3, (January 1937): 103–104. Hutchins then replied in "Grammar, Rhetoric, and Mr. Dewey," *The Social Frontier*, 3, (February 1937): 137–139; and Dewey shot back " 'The Higher Learning in America'," *The Social Frontier*, 3, (March 1937): 167–169. Throughout his succeeding writings on education, Hutchins continued to snipe at what he took to be the fallacies of Deweyan pragmatism. Dewey, for his part, was moved seven years later to reaffirm and elaborate his criticism of Hutchins's ideas in "Challenge to Liberal Thought," *Fortune*, 30, (August 1944): 155.

15. Robert Maynard Hutchins, *Education for Freedom* (Baton Rouge: Louisiana State University Press, 1943), 24.

16. *Ibid.*, 26.

17. Robert Maynard Hutchins, *The Higher Learning in America* (New Haven: Yale University Press, 1936), 97–98.

18. *Ibid.*, 108.

19. Bloom, *The Closing of the American Mind*, 346–347.

20. John Dewey, " 'The Higher Learning in America'," *The Social Frontier*, 3, No. 24 (March 1937): 167.

21. *Ibid.*

22. John Dewey, "Challenge to Liberal Thought," *Fortune*, 30, No. 2 (August 1944): 186.

23. Dewey, " 'The Higher Learning in America'," 167.

24. Richard Rorty, "Hermeneutics, General Studies, and Teaching," *Synergos*, 2 (Fall 1982): 12.

25. Richard Rorty, "That Old-Time Philosophy," *The New Republic*, April 4, 1988, 31.

NOTES TO CHAPTER 2

1. See John Dewey, *Experience and Nature* (New York: Dover, 1958).

2. Hutchins, *Education for Freedom*, 26.

3. Richard Rorty, *Philosophy and the Mirror of Nature* (Princeton: Princeton University Press, 1979).

4. *Ibid.*, 3.

5. *Ibid.*, 3–4.

6. *Ibid.*, 34.

7. *Ibid.*, 35.

8. *Ibid.*, 62.

9. *Ibid.*, 70.

10. *Ibid.*, 71–72.

11. *Ibid.*, 120.

12. *Ibid.*, 126.

13. *Ibid.*, 139–140.

14. *Ibid.*, 140–141, citing T.H. Green, *Hume and Locke* [Green's "Introductions" to Hume's Treatise], ed. Ramon Lemos (New York, 1968), 19.

15. *Ibid.*, 143–144.

16. Friedrich Nietzsche, *The Will to Power*, trans. Walter Kaufmann and R.J. Hollingdale, ed. Walter Kaufmann (New York: Vintage Books, 1967), 307.

17. *Ibid.*, 305.

18. *Ibid.*, 324.

19. Friedrich Nietzsche, *On the Genealogy of Morals*, trans. Walter Kaufmann and R.J. Hollingdale, ed. Walter Kaufmann (New York: Vintage Books, 1967), 95.

20. Walter Benjamin, "Theses on the Philosophy of History," in *Illuminations*, trans. Harry Zorn, ed. Hannah Arendt (New York: Schocken Books, 1968), 256.

21. Nietzsche, *The Will to Power*, 318.

22. Rorty, *Philosophy and the Mirror of Nature*, 147.

23. *Ibid.*, 148.

24. *Ibid.*, 161.

NOTES TO CHAPTER 3

1. Wilfrid Sellars, "Empiricism and the Philosophy of Mind," in *Science, Perception, and Reality* (New York: Humanities Press, 1963).

2. *Ibid.*, 164.

3. *Ibid.*, 169.

4. *Ibid.*, 168.

5. *Ibid.*, 170.

6. *Ibid.*, 176.

7. *Ibid.*, 179.

8. *Ibid.*, 186.

9. *Ibid.*, 187.

10. *Ibid.*, 190.

11. *Ibid.*, 191.

12. *Ibid.*, 194–195.

13. *Ibid.*, 195.

14. See Richard Rorty, "Dewey's Metaphysics," in *Consequences of Pragmatism: (Essays: 1972–1980)* (Minneapolis: University of Minnesota Press, 1982).

15. Sellars, "Empiricism and the Philosophy of Mind," 169.

16. W.V.O. Quine, "Two Dogmas of Empiricism," in *From a Logical Point of View* (Cambridge, MA: Harvard University Press, 1961).

17. *Ibid.*, 20.

18. *Ibid.*, 41.

19. *Ibid.*, 20–21.

20. *Ibid.*, 22.
21. *Ibid.*, 27.
22. *Ibid.*, 31.
23. *Ibid.*, 35.
24. *Ibid.*, 36.
25. *Ibid.*, 36–37.
26. *Ibid.*, 42.
27. *Ibid.*, 43.
28. *Ibid.*, 46.
29. See *ibid.*, 47.
30. Donald Davidson, "On the Very Idea of a Conceptual Scheme," in *Inquiries into Truth and Interpretation* (Oxford: Clarendon Press, 1984).
31. *Ibid.*, 189.
32. Quine, "Two Dogmas of Empiricism," 44.
33. Davidson, "On the Very Idea of a Conceptual Scheme," 189.
34. *Ibid.*, 192.
35. *Ibid.*, 193.
36. *Ibid.*
37. *Ibid.*
38. *Ibid.*, 193–194.
39. See Alfred Tarski, "The Concept of Truth in Formalized Languages," in *Logic, Semantics, Metamathematics* (Oxford: Clarendon Press, 1956).
40. Davidson, "On the Very Idea of a Conceptual Scheme," 194.
41. *Ibid.*
42. Richard Rorty, *Contingency, Irony, and Solidarity* (Cambridge: Cambridge University Press, 1989), 11.
43. *Ibid.*, 11–12.
44. Donald Davidson, "Actions, Reasons, and Causes," in *Actions and Events* (Oxford: Clarendon Press, 1980), 3–4.
45. *Ibid.*, 4.
46. See Michel Foucault, *Discipline and Punish: The Birth of the Prison*, trans. Alan Sheridan (New York: Pantheon Books, 1977).
47. Richard Rorty, *Philosophy and the Mirror of Nature*, 176.
48. *Ibid.*, 179.
49. See G.E. Moore, "Proof of an External World," in *Philosophical Papers* (London: George Allen and Unwin Ltd., 1959).
50. Richard Rorty, *Philosophy and the Mirror of Nature*, 179.
51. *Ibid.*, 317–318.
52. Richard Rorty, "A Reply to Dreyfus and Taylor," *Review of Metaphysics* 34 (September 1980): 52.
53. See Wilfrid Sellars, "Objectivity, Intersubjectivity and the Moral Point of View," chap. 7 of *Science and Metaphysics* (London: Routledge and Kegan Paul Ltd., 1963). Also see W. David Solomon, "Ethical Theory," in C.F. Delaney, Michael J. Loux, Gary Gutting, and W. David Solomon,

The Synoptic Vision: Essays on the Philosophy of Wilfrid Sellars (Notre Dame: University of Notre Dame Press, 1977).

54. Richard Rorty, "Introduction: Pragmatism and Philosophy," in *Consequences of Pragmatism: (Essays: 1972–1980)*, (Minneapolis: University of Minnesota Press, 1982), xlii, citing Jean-Paul Sartre, *L'existentialisme est un humanisme* (Paris: Nagel, 1946), 53–54.

55. See Rorty, *Contingency, Irony, and Solidarity*, 60 and passim.

NOTES TO CHAPTER 4

1. Rorty, *Philosophy and the Mirror of Nature*, 357.
2. *Ibid.*
3. *Ibid.*, 357–358.
4. See Hans-Georg Gadamer, *Truth and Method*, ed. Garrett Barden and John Cumming (New York: Crossroad, 1975), 330–351.
5. Rorty, *Philosophy and the Mirror of Nature*, 358.
6. *Ibid.*, 359.
7. *Ibid.*, 359–360.
8. *Ibid.*, 365.
9. See Gadamer, *Truth and Method*, 267*ff*.
10. Rorty, *Philosophy and the Mirror of Nature*, 366.
11. *Ibid.*, 366–367.
12. *Ibid.*, 367.
13. *Ibid.*, 369–370.
14. See Rorty, *Contingency, Irony, and Solidarity*, 23.
15. *Ibid.*
16. *Ibid.*, 26.
17. Friedrich Nietzsche, *Twilight of the Idols* in *The Portable Nietzsche*, trans. and ed. Walter Kaufmann (New York: Viking Press, 1954), 485–486.
18. *Ibid.*, 485.
19. *Ibid.*
20. Rorty, *Contingency, Irony, and Solidarity*, 27.
21. *Ibid.*, 27–28.
22. See Richard Rorty, "Unfamiliar Noises: Hesse and Davidson on Metaphor" in *Objectivity, Relativism, and Truth: Philosophical Papers*, vol. 1 (Cambridge: Cambridge University Press, 1991), and Donald Davidson, "What Metaphors Mean," in *Inquiries into Truth and Interpretation* (Oxford: Clarendon Press, 1984).
23. Ralph Waldo Emerson, "An Address to the Senior Class in Divinity College, Cambridge, July 15, 1838," in *Ralph Waldo Emerson: Essays and Lectures*, ed. Joel Porte (New York: Literary Classics of the United States, Inc., 1983), 79.

24. See Harold Bloom, *The Anxiety of Influence: A Theory of Poetry* (Oxford: Oxford University Press, 1973).

25. This later terminology is developed in Harold Bloom, *Agon: Towards a Theory of Revisionism* (Oxford: Oxford University Press, 1982).

26. See Sandra M. Gilbert and Susan Gubar, *The Madwoman in the Attic: The Woman Writer and the Nineteenth-Century Literary Imagination* (New Haven: Yale University Press, 1979), 46–53.

27. See Richard Rorty, "Feminism and Pragmatism," *Michigan Quarterly Review* 30 (Spring 1991): 321–358.

28. Rorty, *Contingency, Irony, and Solidarity*, 29.

29. See Donald Davidson, "Mental Events," in *Actions and Events* (Oxford: Oxford University Press, 1980).

30. See Ludwig Wittgenstein, *Philosophical Investigations*, trans. G.E.M. Anscombe, 3d ed. (New York: The Macmillan Company, 1958), 91–97.

31. Rorty, *Contingency, Irony, and Solidarity*, 29.

32. Richard Rorty, "The Priority of Democracy to Philosophy," in *Objectivity, Relativism, and Truth: Philosophical Papers*, vol. 1 (Cambridge: Cambridge University Press, 1991), 191.

33. Rorty, *Contingency, Irony, and Solidarity*, 36.

34. Ludwig Wittgenstein, *Tractatus Logico-Philosophicus*, trans. D.F. Pears and B.F. McGuiness, with an Introduction by Bertrand Russell (London: Routledge and Kegan Paul Ltd., 1961), 117.

35. *Ibid.*

36. *Ibid.*, 115.

37. See Immanuel Kant, "What is Enlightenment?" in *Foundations of the Metaphysics of Morals and What is Enlightenment?* trans., with an Introduction by, Lewis White Beck (Indianapolis: The Bobbs-Merrill Company, Inc., 1959).

38. Richard Rorty, "Freud and Moral Reflection," in *Essays on Heidegger and Others: Philosophical Papers*, vol. 2 (Cambridge: Cambridge University Press, 1991), 152.

39. *Ibid.*, 154.

40. *Ibid.*, 155.

41. *Ibid.*

42. Rorty, *Philosophy and the Mirror of Nature*, 394.

NOTES TO CHAPTER 5

1. Rorty, "That Old-Time Philosophy," 31.

2. Rorty is echoing here Hans Blumenberg's account of how modern European culture developed out of the transvaluation of curiosity from a vice to a virtue. See Hans Blumenberg, *The Legitimacy of the Modern Age*, trans. Robert M. Wallace (Cambridge, MA: The MIT Press, 1983), 227–453.

3. Bloom, *The Closing of the American Mind*, 38.
4. Rorty, "That Old-Time Philosophy," 30.
5. Rorty, "Hermeneutics, General Studies, and Teaching," 9–10.
6. *Ibid.*, 10–11.
7. *Ibid.*, 13.
8. Rorty, *Contingency, Irony, and Solidarity*, 73.
9. *Ibid.*, 73–74.
10. *Ibid.*, 74.
11. *Ibid.*, 89–90.
12. *Ibid.*, 87.
13. *Ibid.*, 91–92.
14. See Thomas Mann, *Doctor Faustus*, trans. H.T. Lowe-Porter (New York: Alfred A. Knopf, 1965).
15. See Rorty's response to Habermas's work in Rorty, *Contingency, Irony, and Solidarity*, 65–69.
16. *Ibid.*, 93.
17. *Ibid.*, 92.
18. See Nel Noddings, *Caring: A Feminine Approach to Ethics and Moral Education* (Berkeley: University of California Press, 1984).
19. See Thomas S. Kuhn, *The Structure of Scientific Revolutions*, 2d ed. (Chicago: The University of Chicago Press, 1970), Paul Feyerabend, *Against Method: Outline of an Anarchistic Theory of Knowledge* (London: Verso, 1975), and Jean-François Lyotard, *The Differend: Phrases in Dispute*, trans. Georges Van Den Abbeele (Minneapolis: University of Minnesota Press, 1988).
20. See Sebastiano Timpanaro, *On Materialism*, trans. Lawrence Garner (London: Verso, 1975) and Foucault, *Discipline and Punish*.
21. Stanley Cavell, *The Claim of Reason: Wittgenstein, Skepticism, Morality, and Tragedy* (Oxford: Oxford University Press, 1979), 430.
22. Ernesto Laclau and Chantal Mouffe, *Hegemony and Socialist Strategy: Towards a Radical Democratic Politics*, trans. Winston Moore and Paul Cammack (London: Verso, 1985).
23. Ernesto Laclau, "Community and Its Paradoxes: Richard Rorty's 'Liberal Utopia'," in *Community at Loose Ends*, ed. The Miami Theory Collective (Minneapolis: University of Minnesota Press, 1991).
24. *Ibid.*, 95.
25. *Ibid.*, 95–96.
26. See Foucault, *Discipline and Punish*.

NOTES TO CHAPTER 6

1. See Jonas F. Soltis, "Introduction," in *Philosophy and Education*, ed. by Jonas F. Soltis (Chicago: The University of Chicago Press, 1981).
2. Jean-Baptiste Poquelin Molière, *The Misanthrope and Tartuffe*,

trans. by Richard Wilbur (New York: Harcourt Brace Jovanovich, 1965), 152.

3. Stanley Cavell, "A Cover Letter to Molière's *Misanthrope*," in *Themes out of School: Effects and Causes* (San Francisco: North Point Press, 1984), 98.

4. *Ibid.*, 102.

5. *Ibid.*, 98.

6. *Ibid.*

7. *Ibid.*

8. For an insightful discussion of Rousseau's concept, see Charles Taylor, *The Ethics of Authenticity* (Cambridge, MA: Harvard University Press, 1991), 27.

9. Cavell, "A Cover Letter to Molière's *Misanthrope*," 100.

10. *Ibid.*

11. *Ibid.*

12. *Ibid.*, 99–100.

13. *Ibid.*, 98–99.

14. *Ibid.*, 105.

15. *Ibid.*, 101.

16. See Stanley Cavell, "Foreword: An Audience for Philosophy," in *Must We Mean What We Say? A Book of Essays* (Cambridge: Cambridge University Press, 1969).

WORKS CITED

Benjamin, Walter. "Theses on the Philosophy of History," in *Illuminations,* translated by Harry Zorn, edited by Hannah Arendt. New York:
Schocken Books, 1968.

Bloom, Allan. *The Closing of the American Mind: How Higher Education
Has Failed Democracy and Impoverished the Souls of Today's Students,*
with a Foreword by Saul Bellow. New York: Simon and Schuster, Inc.,
1987.

Bloom, Harold. *The Anxiety of Influence: A Theory of Poetry.* Oxford:
Oxford University Press, 1973.

———. *Agon: Towards a Theory of Revisionism.* Oxford: Oxford University
Press, 1982.

Blumenberg, Hans. *The Legitimacy of the Modern Age,* translated by Robert
M. Wallace. Cambridge, MA: The MIT Press, 1983.

Cavell, Stanley. "Foreword: An Audience for Philosophy," in *Must We
Mean What We Say? A Book of Essays.* Cambridge: Cambridge University Press, 1969.

———. *The Claim of Reason: Wittgenstein, Skepticism, Morality, and
Tragedy.* Oxford: Oxford University Press, 1979.

———. "A Cover Letter to Molière's *Misanthrope,*" in *Themes out of
School: Effects and Causes.* San Francisco: North Point Press, 1984.

———. "Who Disappoints Whom?" *Critical Inquiry* 15 (Spring 1989):
606–610.

———. *Conditions Handsome and Unhandsome: The Constitution of
Emersonian Perfectionism: The Carus Lectures, 1988.* Chicago: The
University of Chicago Press, 1990.

Davidson, Donald. "Actions, Reasons, and Causes," in *Actions and Events.*
Oxford: Clarendon Press, 1980.

———. "Mental Events," in *Actions and Events.* Oxford: Clarendon Press,
1980.

———. "On the Very Idea of a Conceptual Scheme," in *Inquiries into
Truth and Interpretation.* Oxford: Clarendon Press, 1984.

————. "What Metaphors Mean," in *Inquiries into Truth and Interpretation*. Oxford: Clarendon Press, 1984.

Descartes, René. *Discourse on Method and Meditations on First Philosophy*, translated by Donald A. Cress. Indianapolis: Hackett, 1980.

Dewey, John. *Democracy and Education: An Introduction to the Philosophy of Education*. New York: The Free Press, 1916.

————. "Rationality in Education." *The Social Frontier* 3 (December 1936): 71–73.

————. "President Hutchins' Proposals to Remake Higher Education." *The Social Frontier* 3 (January 1937): 103–104.

————. " 'The Higher Learning in America.' " *The Social Frontier* 3 (March 1937): 167–169.

————. "Challenge to Liberal Thought." *Fortune* 30 (August 1944): 155.

————. *Experience and Nature*. New York: Dover Publications, 1958.

Emerson, Ralph Waldo. "An Address to the Senior Class in Divinity College, Cambridge, July 15, 1838," in *Essays and Lectures*, edited by Joel Porte. New York: Literary Classics of the United States, Inc., 1983.

Feyerabend, Paul. *Against Method: Outline of an Anarchistic Theory of Knowledge*. London: Verso, 1975.

Foucault, Michel. *Discipline and Punish: The Birth of the Prison*, translated by Alan Sheridan. New York: Pantheon Books, 1977.

Gadamer, Hans-Georg. *Truth and Method*, edited by Garrett Barden and John Cumming. New York: Crossroad, 1975.

Gilbert, Sandra M., and Susan Gubar. *The Madwoman in the Attic: The Woman Writer and the Nineteenth-Century Literary Imagination*. New Haven: Yale University Press, 1979.

Hutchins, Robert Maynard. *The Higher Learning in America*. New Haven: Yale University Press, 1936.

————. "Grammar, Rhetoric, and Mr. Dewey." *The Social Frontier* 3 (February 1937): 137–139.

————. *Education for Freedom*. Baton Rouge: Louisiana State University Press, 1943.

Kant, Immanuel. *Foundations of the Metaphysics of Morals and What is Enlightenment?* translated, with an Introduction, by Lewis White Beck. Indianapolis: The Bobbs-Merrill Company, Inc., 1959.

Kuhn, Thomas A. *The Structure of Scientific Revolutions*. 2d ed. Chicago: The University of Chicago Press, 1970.

Laclau, Ernesto. "Community and Its Paradoxes: Richard Rorty's 'Liberal Utopia'," in *Community at Loose Ends*, edited by The Miami Theory Collective. Minneapolis: University of Minnesota Press, 1991.

Laclau, Ernesto, and Chantal Mouffe. *Hegemony and Socialist Strategy: Towards a Radical Democratic Politics*, translated by Winston Moore and Paul Cammack. London: Verso, 1985.

Lyotard, Jean-François. *The Differend: Phrases in Dispute*, translated by George Van Den Abbeele. Minneapolis: University of Minnesota Press, 1988.

Mann, Thomas. *Doctor Faustus*, translated by H.T. Lowe-Porter. New York: Alfred A. Knopf, 1965.

Molière, Jean-Baptiste Poquelin. *The Misanthrope and Tartuffe*, translated by Richard Wilbur. New York: Harcourt Brace Jovanovich, 1965.

Moore, G.E. "Proof of an External World," in *Philosophical Papers*. London: George Allen and Unwin, Ltd., 1959.

Nietzsche, Friedrich. *Twilight of the Idols*, in *The Portable Nietzsche*, translated and edited by Walter Kaufmann. New York: Viking Press, 1954.

———. *On the Genealogy of Morals*, translated by Walter Kaufmann and R.J. Hollingdale, edited by Walter Kaufmann. New York: Vintage Books, 1967.

———. *The Will to Power*, translated by Walter Kaufmann and R.J. Hollingdale, edited by Walter Kaufmann. New York: Vintage Books, 1967.

Noddings, Nel. *Caring: A Feminine Approach to Ethics and Moral Education*. Berkeley: University of California Press, 1984.

Oakeshott, Michael. "A Place of Learning," in *The Voice of Liberal Learning: Michael Oakeshott on Education*, edited by Timothy Fuller. New Haven: Yale University Press, 1989.

———. "The Study of Politics in a University," in *Rationalism in Politics and Other Essays*, with a Foreword by Timothy Fuller. New and expanded ed. Indianapolis: Liberty Press, 1991.

Plato. *The Collected Dialogues of Plato Including the Letters*, edited by Edith Hamilton and Huntington Cairns. Princeton: Princeton University Press, 1961.

Quine, W.V.O. "Two Dogmas of Empiricism," in *From a Logical Point of View*. Cambridge, MA: Harvard University Press, 1961.

Rorty, Richard. *Philosophy and the Mirror of Nature*. Princeton: Princeton University Press, 1979.

———. "A Reply to Dreyfus and Taylor." *Review of Metaphysics* 34 (September 1980): 39–46.

———. "Hermeneutics, General Studies, and Teaching." *Synergos* 2 (Fall 1982): 1–15.

———. "Dewey's Metaphysics," in *Consequences of Pragmatism: (Essays: 1972–1980)*. Minneapolis: University of Minnesota Press, 1982.

———. "Introduction: Pragmatism and Philosophy," in *Consequences of Pragmatism: (Essays: 1972–1980)*. Minneapolis: University of Minnesota Press, 1982.

———. "That Old-Time Philosophy." *The New Republic*, (April 4, 1988): 28–33.

———. *Contingency, Irony, and Solidarity*. Cambridge: Cambridge University Press, 1989.

———. "Feminism and Pragmatism." *Michigan Quarterly Review* 30 (Spring 1991): 231–258.

———. "The Priority of Democracy to Philosophy," in *Objectivism, Rela-*

tivism, and Truth: Philosophical Papers, vol. 1. Cambridge: Cambridge University Press, 1991.

————. "Unfamiliar Noises: Hesse and Davidson on Metaphor," in *Objectivism, Relativism, and Truth: Philosophical Papers*, vol. 1. Cambridge: Cambridge University Press, 1991.

————. "Freud and Moral Reflection," in *Essays on Heidegger and Others: Philosophical Papers*, vol. 2. Cambridge: Cambridge University Press, 1991.

Sellars, Wilfrid. "Empiricism and the Philosophy of Mind," in *Science, Perception, and Reality*. New York: Humanities Press, 1963.

————. "Objectivity, Intersubjectivity and the Moral Point of View." Chap. 7 of *Science and Metaphysics*. London: Routledge and Kegan Paul, Ltd., 1968.

Solomon, W. David. "Ethical Theory," in C.F. Delaney, Michael J. Loux, Gary Gutting, and W. David Solomon, *The Synoptic Vision: Essays on the Philosophy of Wilfrid Sellars*. Notre Dame: University of Notre Dame Press, 1977.

Soltis, Jonas F. "Introduction," in *Philosophy and Education*, edited by Jonas F. Soltis. Chicago: The University of Chicago Press, 1981.

Tarski, Alfred. "The Concept of Truth in Formalized Languages," in *Logic, Semantics, Metamathematics*. Oxford: Clarendon Press, 1956.

Taylor, Charles. *The Ethics of Authenticity*. Cambridge, MA: Harvard University Press, 1991.

Timpanaro, Sebastiano. *On Materialism*, translated by Lawrence Garner. London: Verso, 1975.

Wittgenstein, Ludwig. *Philosophical Investigations*, translated by G.E.M. Anscombe. 3d ed. New York: The Macmillan Company, 1958.

————. *Tractatus Logico-Philosophicus*, translated by D.F. Pears and B.F. McGuinness, with an Introduction by Bertrand Russell. London: Routledge and Kegan Paul, Ltd., 1961.

INDEX

nihilism of, 35, 48, 73, 104, 110; and personhood, 21, 48; as a radical ironist, 122; and reason, 21, 48, 73; and resentment, 44, 48, 108; and "true world," 90–92; and will to power, xii, 21, 40–45, 48, 72–73, 103–104

Noddings, Nel, 116

O

Oakeshott, Michael, 3–5, 75, 105, 151

P

Plato: and allegory of the cave, 107; and eroticism, 9, 109; and first principles, 14; influence of Socrates on, 19, 106; and learning how to die, 90; metaphysics of, xii–xiii, 105; and realm of ideal forms, 10–11; and Socrates as a teacher, 3–4; and "true world," 91, 98

Ptolemy, 63

Q

Quine, W. V. O.: critique of analyticity, 50, 58–62, 65; Davidson's critique of, 64–65, 69–70; holistic view of knowledge, 62–64; influence on Rorty, 21, 50

R

Rorty, Richard, 151; and acculturation, 85, 87–88; and aims of liberal education, 108; and alternative vocabularies, 70–71; challenges to philosophy of liberal education of, 110–130 passim; and conflict between ironic edification and conversational solidarity, 123; and conversational edification, 105, 107–109, 114, 130–132, 150–151, 153–154; and criticism of one's culture, 73–74; critique of analytical philosophy, ix, x; critique of Descartes' notion of "the mind," 30–36; critique

of Kant's notion of mental synthesis, 50; critique of Locke's theory of knowledge, 35–39, 58; critique of metaphysics in liberal education, 19–22, 26–27, 102; critique of positivism, x; and Davidson's theory of truth, 50, 64–70; and Dewey's antimetaphysical arguments, 19–22, 26–27, 131; and dominance of epistemology, xi, 26–28, 47; and edification, 83–88, 98–102, 119, 124, 127; and eroticism in liberal education, 19, 109; and exploration of other cultures, 107, 110, 114; and hermeneutics, 74–76, 81–82, 84–85; and history of ideas, xiii, 28–47 passim, 89; and human susceptibility to pain, 121–123; influence of Heidegger on, xii; influence of Nietzsche on, 21, 40, 103–104; influence of Socrates on, 19, 105–106; and intellectual authority, 21; and Kant's critique of Enlightenment theory of knowledge, 46–47, 58; and liberal ironists, 22, 111–116, 122, 135, 150; and metaphors, 93; and moral perfectionism, 23, 102; and Nietzsche's critique of Enlightenment theory of knowledge, 45–48, 72–73, 103–104; and philosophical education for cultural reform, 79–80, 103, 105, 130; and public-private distinctions, 123–127, 129–130, 153; and Quine's critique of analyticity, 50, 65; and reason, 73, 78, 103, 105; and reformulation of personhood (selfhood), 79–83, 89–90, 92, 94–105; and Sellars's critique of the Myth of the Given, 50, 57–58; and tension between explanation and justification, 48–50, 58, 65, 71–73; and "true world," 90–92; and "we-intentions," 76–78

Rousseau, Jean-Jacques, 117, 138